Spir

What Matters — and What Doesn't

Revised Edition

Helen Hills

iUniverse, Inc.

New York Lincoln Shanghai

Spiritual Living
What Matters — and What Doesn't

iUniverse, Inc.

For information address:
iUniverse, Inc.
2021 Pine Lake Road, Suite 100
Lincoln, NE 68512
www.iuniverse.com

ISBN: 0-595-29454-5 (pbk)
ISBN: 0-595-66001-0 (cloth)

Printed in the United States of America

To each of my children

ACKNOWLEDGEMENTS

Special thanks have been earned by the discussion groups of the West Avon Congregational Church in Avon, Conn., and the Charlemont Federated Church in Charlemont, Mass. The suggestions of these two groups have been helpful, particularly in the choice and phrasing of discussion questions at the end of each chapter. Their comments on the liveliness of discussion that the book sparked were very encouraging. I also wish to acknowledge with gratitude the varied contributions of Linda Comstock, friend and ally in my various writing projects.

I am deeply grateful to Brian Wiprud, who designed the cover and helped me with computer transmission; Ted Wiprud, whose language expertise improved the phrasing of this book; and Rebecca Wiprud and Mary Owen, whose editorial comments were incorporated early on. My husband as usual backed me in my efforts.

Contents

Full bibliographical information appears at the end of this book for all bracketed citations after quotations. A title is given only when more than one book by an author is cited, and then it is abbreviated. Biblical quotations are from the Revised Standard Version, 1946.

INTRODUCTION

If you have picked up this book and opened it to this page, I may reasonably assume that you are aware that life has a spiritual dimension. Further, I may take one step more and suppose that you are searching for a fuller experience of that dimension. Aren't we all, no matter how fulfilled we may feel ourselves at times!

In this book, I attempt to respond to common dilemmas that we "spiritual seekers" face in these times and in this culture. The first has to do with the language of both spirituality and religion, including the word "God." The name immediately conjures up an old man sitting grandly "up there," no matter how often we tell ourselves that we have long ago outgrown such a visualization. Then what about the "he" and "she" of God? I deal with these issues in chapter one.

Next comes the matter of believing in this "God," or whatever we are calling him or her. How do we do this? You remember the often quoted, "I believe; help thou my unbelief." We know what the man meant. Chapter two discusses belief.

I shall not enumerate all the problems, which you can guess from a glance at the table of contents. However, I shall name an important few that face us all in this century, whether we are agnostic, Jewish, Christian, Buddhist, or of any other persuasion. How should we pray? How can a loving God allow or perhaps perpetrate disasters? Why does he permit evil? Is attending and belonging to a religious congregation necessary to spiritual wellbeing? Isn't loving our fellow creature and actively trying to help the needy sufficient, without any belief in anything at all? Was Jesus the Son of God, whatever that means? How can we live a more spiritually fulfilling life? All these questions tumble out of our minds, and often they form the basis of long, theological discussions. The only such question no longer discussed (and I have read that it never actually was!) is how many angels can fit on the head of a pin. You will notice, however, that I do have something to say about angels in the last chapter, but without answering that question.

My responses are all of the commonsense variety. They are based on my own experiences and thinking, as well as my considerable reading about those of other people. Along the way, I describe various types and stages of spiritual experience and suggest approaches that may be productive in increasing our realization and enjoyment of our spiritual life.

Above all, I try to distinguish between what matters and what doesn't. A friend of mine, somewhat younger than I, remarked the other day that the longer she lives the more she realizes that most of the issues that cause distress, discussion, and argument "just don't matter." I nodded, we talked about a few other things, I departed, and then I started to think about what she had said. And lo and behold, she had given me the subtitle for this book.

Not only are there many questions whose answers, such as they may be, do not really matter. There are also contradictions, paradoxes, dilemmas in this life that we humans are not up to understanding. Picture the tremendous universe, galaxies upon galaxies, black holes, curved space, and the rest of it. Now, way down at the bottom of your mental picture, place a tiny dot on a small planet. Is it likely that this dot can indeed fathom the mysteries of everything else? Some dots think they can. I disagree, as you will discover, and I am not alone.

A third tenet underlying this book is that one size does *not* fit all. We are all different, each of us is unique, and—isn't that wonderful.

I hope you will find this book helpful in moving toward a full blooming of your spiritual life, and that you will enjoy reading it as much as I have enjoyed writing it.

1

SPIRITUALITY and LANGUAGE

> It is all but impossible to describe the new awareness that comes when words are abandoned.... Words can enhance experience, but they can also take so much away. We see an insect and at once we abstract certain characteristics and classify it—a fly. And in that very cognitive exercise, part of the wonder is gone.... Words are part of our rational selves, and to abandon them for a while is to give freer reign to our intuitive selves. [Goodall, 79]

Who or what is this entity or being that we call God? And is this question sufficiently relevant to daily living to be seriously considered by mature adults in the twenty-first century? Or has it become merely an endless exercise in logic and debate, appropriate to adolescents, clergy, and others who have become "religious"? Might we not be better served by concerning ourselves with what is currently termed "spirituality," which is less tainted by tradition and institutions?

Spirituality is variously defined, having the attraction of vagueness. We can adapt it easily to our own experience. Theologian Thomas Hart calls it "that nebulous reality which has caught the popular imagination." [Hart, 5] Jungian therapist Jeremiah Abrams describes spirituality as "a holy longing, a yearning to know the meaning of our lives, to have a connection with the transpersonal." [quoted by Hart, 39] I like this definition, because it resonates with the deeper experiences of all but the most callow or superficial person.

Spirituality may or may not lead to religion. Hart calls it "religion's root." Spirituality can be said to become what we term "religion" at the moment when it names God as its focus. William James would not even require the naming. He writes: "Were one asked to characterize the life of religion in the broadest and most general terms possible, one might say that it consists of the belief that there is an unseen order, and that our supreme good lies in harmoniously adjusting ourselves thereto." [James, 59] James characterizes the goal of religion from the point of view not of a believer, but of a searcher: "Does God really exist? How does he exist? What is he? are so many irrelevant questions. Not God, but life, more life, a larger, richer, more satisfying life, is, in the last analysis the end of religion. The love of life, at any and every level of development, is the religious impulse." [James, 392]

It is the naming that causes difficulties for many people. Language is the source of major difficulties and misunderstandings in spiritual and religious matters. While it is our most important and precise way of communicating with each other, language sometimes becomes the primary source of significant miscommunication. This has happened to the word "God."

What we must remember is that a word is a symbol, not the reality, and if everyone understands what it symbolizes, well and good. However, in the field of spiritual experience, we are not dealing with tangible objects. We cannot touch, hear, smell, taste, or see a spiritual experience. Furthermore, words tend to accumulate bits of this and that as they are used throughout the years, so that sometimes the baggage they carry almost completely hides their original meaning.

The language of spiritual experience is particularly vulnerable to misunderstanding. Many words have lost their original meaning or the meaning has been distorted by long, sometimes careless, and always culturally vulnerable use. This distortion occurs with almost any word related to spiritual and particularly religious experience. For examples, start with "God," move to "belief," and then perhaps "salvation." How about "heaven," "soul," and "hell"? And on and on. I am quite certain that any three or four people would come up with an equal number of definitions, and also that most of us would not even try to clarify the meanings of such words nor expect everyone else to agree with our own definitions.

However, at certain periods of history there *was* considerable agreement on the definition of the words mentioned above. Concepts formulated to understand spiritual experiences were more generally understood than they are today, although they may not always have been meaningful in everyday spiritual life. There is something about the human mind that cannot resist picking up ideas and arranging them in a clever schema. Many of us like to organize everything into outlines with all parts related to each other, so that we can say, "Well, that's done. I understand all about that." And then we can brush our hands together, nod sagely, drop the subject, and turn to the next topic in need of our organization. The intellectual discipline of analysis and synthesis is fine and dandy—in fact very useful—as long as the original meaning of the symbols is not lost, which is what can happen, and indeed has happened, when terms related to spiritual experience are used by those who have little idea of what the symbols originally stood for.

I would like to take a large, clean eraser and move it across the blackboard on which theologies have been written. I would like to start all over again and write just one word to designate the "element" that spiritual experiences share and leave it at that. Although, as recorded throughout the ages, such experiences differ almost as much as the individual people who have had them, they do share an "element" other than ourself that is known as active, definitely personal, and usually powerful. It is most natural to me to use the word "God," because I have been brought up and remain within the Judeo-Christian tradition, but the word carries connotations that are "off-putting" to the many agnostics who have rejected that tradition. I am tempted to keep one of the last words written just recently on the very edge of the blackboard, "the Force," because it has been disassociated with the others on the board, but unfortunately it brings with it the distracting aura of science fiction. No matter what word I choose, it will have a barnacle or two.

My dilemma is what word to use that will not throw off a reader who has declared himself or herself an agnostic or atheist, but is aware of life's spiritual dimension. I know that to this person the word "God" produces negative vibrations. Watts puts the situation more strongly as "acquired repugnant emotional associations." [Watts, 109] On the other hand, the person who has not reacted against religion will be annoyed by a coy evasion and consider me timorous and unaffirming if I sidestep the name. I would like to go way back to the original meaning of the name of the Hebrew God, "I am that I am," but that is a bit *more* than awkward. So let us not discard the word "God," which carries so much positive meaning for many deeply spiritual people, but let us add upon occasion other names that may be more descriptive in a particular context and less negative to those who find themselves antagonized by traditional and organized religion. The words "the Spirit," "the Mystery," and "the Ground of Being" somehow remove our childlike vision of God in a white robe up there in the sky and replace it with the idea of a largely unknowable presence that corresponds more easily with our spiritual experiences in everyday life. I will, however, continue to use the name "God," particularly when discussing the Spirit in its biblical or distinctly Christian context. As Thomas Hart suggests, it may be best "to work on refurbishing the *images* and *concepts* with which it is linked," [Hart, 33] rather than discarding it.

A further problem is the personal pronoun. The Spirit is experienced as neither exclusively male nor female, but most certainly not as an impersonal "it." Religious traditions throughout world history have recognized that the deity comprises female as well as male. Only recently, however, has the female aspect of the Christian God become a matter for discussion and usually emphasis. Corresponding with the emergence of feminism, a writer is hard put to avoid "he/she" for either an individual person or the Spirit. I try to avoid sentence structures that make a decision on this point necessary, but having been raised in a tradition where "mankind" and "he" both could safely be assumed to be either male or female, depending upon context, I may at times—in fact at *most* times—yield to the masculine pronoun. May my editor and also feminists (of both the masculine and feminine genders) forgive me!

Back to the central issue of who or what God is and the relevance of that question. First, it must be said that God is who he is, regardless of what we think he is. An obvious statement, perhaps, but one that needs to be made. I have noticed, with some wry amusement, that those who declare that there is no God—presumably meaning at least a supreme being, creator of the universe—seem to feel a sense of relief, as if they have courageously just swept away an imaginary dragon. Meanwhile, they forget that they just may be wrong, and that the imaginary dragon may in fact be real and not exactly as they have imagined; and that their declaration that he doesn't exist has not in fact done away with him. They are like a man sitting on the back of an elephant while declaring that there is no such animal as an elephant. One might add that image to the usual one of blind men, each touching a different part of the elephant and erroneously concluding that his own version of the total animal is the correct one.

The reason for the dismissal of God varies, but often has to do with unfortunate experiences with organized religions. An example of this that comes to mind occurred some years ago, on a Christmas Eve. A young woman sharing our family's Christmas Eve dinner proclaimed that she did not wish to attend Christian services that evening because she no longer believed in God and did not wish to be hypocritical. She explained that she had lost her belief in God because as a young child she had gone to parochial school, for various reasons had not liked the school, and as a result of her experiences there had discarded religion. She was in effect saying that her personal experience as a child had wiped God out of the universe. And I have run into many another so-called atheist since that time who has drawn equally illogical conclusions. One cannot prove a negative.

My second observation about the nature of God is equally obvious, I fear, but nevertheless necessary—namely, that no one of us can ever answer completely the question of who and what God is. Augustine said this well: "Before experiencing God you thought you could talk about God; when you begin to experience God you realize that what you are experiencing you cannot put into words." [quoted by Borg, *God*, 48] Throughout our lives, we are in the process of discovering God more fully, each of us in our own way. Paul Tillich points to God as the "infinite and inexhaustible depth and ground of all being." [Hart, 19] Essayist and university teacher Scott Russell Sanders, reaching for a description, writes: "By mystery I do not mean simply the blank places on our maps. I mean the divine source—not a void, not a darkness, but an uncapturable fullness. We are sustained by processes and powers that we can neither fathom nor do without." [Sanders, 162]

Thomas Hart attempts a "new description" of God, summarized as "an invisible center of energy, vitality, creativity, and love at the core of everything." [Hart, 20] He continues by suggesting that we discard our childish Sunday school version and view God in eight ways, as: the Source of reality; the Object of our deepest longing; the Assurance of meaning, value, purpose; the Depth in things, the Mystery in the background; the Power on which we rely; the Font of beauty, goodness, truth, love; the Silent Presence deep within us; and the Call to do the good, to be responsible. Summing up, Hart says that we find God in "the heart and center of all reality." I particularly like a quotation by Thomas Merton:

> Life is this simple. We are living in a world that is absolutely transparent, and God is shining through it all the time. This is not just a fable or a nice story. It is true. If we abandon ourselves to God and forget ourselves, we see it sometimes, and we see it maybe frequently. God shows Himself everywhere, in everything—in people

like I did on my walk this a.m. 12/27/07.
@ Bolton Valley.

and in things and in nature and in events. It becomes very obvious that God is everywhere and in everything and we cannot be without Him. It's impossible. The only thing is that we don't see it. [quoted by Borg, *Jesus,* 47]

The relevance of a God so defined to anyone who is living life with any depth at all is clear. Whenever we dip below the surface of life, we run into a something, a Mystery, a Spirit, who has been called God.

So, why does the language seem to remain much the same even for those who are intellectually aware that God is not that bearded old man in the sky but a Spirit, the Mystery, the Ground of our Being? Why do the theologians who understand him in this very spiritual way seem to "fall" into anthropomorphic language as soon as they are discussing other matters? The answer is frustrating, but true—because that is the way our minds are made. Bishop Spong puts this fact vividly:

> Are we not aware of that ancient bit of folk wisdom suggesting that "if horses had gods they would look like horses"? No creature can finally conceptualize beyond its own limits or its own being. A horse cannot think or imagine beyond the experience of a horse. Despite our human pretensions, that is also true of human beings. If human beings have gods, they will look and act remarkably like human beings. None of us can ever get beyond that. If we are going to speak of God at all, we must begin by acknowledging that limitation. [Spong, 47]

Our language makes God into a person, which is upsetting to many people, particularly those who are having trouble discarding their childhood images. However, when we read about God or hear someone speak of him, all we need do is remind ourselves of the spiritual concept of God and in effect make an instantaneous translation from the anthropomorphic God that our language demands into the spiritual being whom we meet in our everyday life and about whom we are continually learning. Spong thinks that this can happen because the "experience of God as the Ground of Being has a way of breaking open every human word and making it usable again." [Spong, 225] Spong, for whom the idea of an external and personal God is particularly troubling, tries to handle this in a rather muddy fashion by writing of "the God who is not a personal being but who is made known in the personal being of the whole creation." [Spong, 196] The final word and warning on this subject to my mind was written by C. S. Lewis, whose perceptions of human weaknesses equaled his awareness of God's presence in our lives:

> But never…let us think that while anthropomorphic images are a concession to our weakness, the abstractions are the literal truth.… It will make the life of lives inanimate and the love of loves impersonal. The *naif* image is mischievous chiefly in so far as it holds unbelievers back from conversion. It does believers, even at its crudest, no harm. What soul ever perished for believing that God the Father really has a beard? [Lewis, *Prayer,* 21-22]

It usually does not matter whether the writer or speaker has exactly the same spiritualized concept that we have, and often it is difficult to know. So I will usually simply use the term God and also the masculine pronoun, trusting the reader to translate. Our language and the way our minds work demand a personalization of some sort.

Because we each have our own set of genes and live different lives, we discover God in different ways and times. And if we could collect all the discoveries about God that have been made by all sentient beings, from the very beginning to the very end of the universe, we would come closer to a concept of God than we possibly can individually. Remember the elephant and the blind men, each of whom perceived a separate part of the elephant and thus described it differently. Not only was each man's version of the elephant wrong, but the composite picture from all of the men's versions was pretty close to right. Such partial discoveries about God abound, the Bible being one of them. The more we read or hear about others' revelations and discoveries, the more likely we are to perceive and experience those aspects of God in our own lives, and the richer our lives will become. We can gradually learn to find the gold even in the religious terms that may at first seem outdated and irrelevant. This happened to Kathleen Norris and in fact led toward her conversion to the Christian faith. She writes: "In may ways, it is my accommodation of and reconciliation with the vocabulary of Christian faith that has been the measure of my conversion, the way in which I have entered and now claim the faith as my own." [Norris, 6]

The first step, however, is to ignore the language and concepts that say nothing significant to us in our everyday lives, admit that we cannot fully understand everything about God and our world, and then recognize that to live well and happily we do not need answers to all our questions. Many do not really matter to the quality of our lives. We then become free to build. We can look down into the depths of ourselves and of all Being and begin to encounter the Mystery. We may later find that new meanings will emerge from some of the old language and concepts that will enrich our spiritual lives.

Not only may outdated language and complex concepts become unimportant, but many seemingly unsolvable problems may also begin to disappear. The first we usually face is the basic matter of *belief*. What do we really believe about God/the Mystery/the Ground of Being? Is it even necessary to "believe in" God, in the usual sense? And how can we come to belief, if this is what we think necessary? This "belief problem," the subject of the next chapter, is also partially a matter of language.

DISCUSSION QUESTIONS

How does "spirituality" differ from religion? Is it "religion's root"?

Do you find that words hinder the expression of spiritual experience or do they help you define it and render it communicable? Or a combination of hindering and helping?

What comes to your mind when you hear the word "God"? Is there another term that is more meaningful to you?

Do you think "God" is in this world in a personal way?

Have you had experiences that turn you away from the Christian religion? If so, what were they?

2

BELIEF and FAITH

Today, many intelligent people hesitate to speak of God at all, because they can no longer believe in God—the God, that is, that they were raised with. They would not call themselves atheists, and are often quite interested in spirituality, but the God of their childhood has faded from view entirely and nothing more adequate has come to replace "Him." When they think about it, they wonder if they believe at all. [Hart, 17]

I would like to see the omnipresent word "belief," along with its verb "to believe," erased from the language of religion. In current popular usage, it means not quite knowing something intellectually but choosing to take a chance that it is true. It combines thought and desire with a persistent element of uncertainty. It often involves a yearning for certainty and at times a determination that the uncertain be swallowed whole and assumed certain. The prevalence of the distress caused by this situation is reflected in our familiarity with the cry of the father bringing his child to Jesus for healing, "I believe; help my unbelief!" [Mark 9:24]

The underlying problem is that, try as we may, we cannot force ourselves to believe that something exists or that something is true. Our inability often results in persistent and sometimes agonizing attempts over the years, with consequent guilt or pretense. Annie Dillard writes at length and vividly about those of us who are following the "spiritual path," which she calls "the hilarious popular term for those nightblind mesas and flayed hills in which people grope, for decades on end, with the goal of knowing the absolute.... Year after year they find themselves still feeling with their fingers for lumps in the dark." [Dillard, 86-87] Or, if we acknowledge that we have been unable to believe, we may quite illogically jump to the conclusion that whatever we were trying to believe or believe in does not exist or is not true. Most important, no matter how we stand in the matter of belief, the very concept of belief may block our experience of God (or the Spirit).

What does that phrase "believe in" really mean? Is it like believing in Santa Claus, the Easter Bunny, and the Tooth Fairy? Early on, we learn that they don't really exist in the way that we thought they did, as creatures who could be glimpsed if we were only able to be present at the just the right moment. We are told by our parents that they had not lied to us, because the picturesque trio have a spiritual existence more important than a physical one. (I am not sure the Tooth Fairy is included in this explanation, but it might be.) Many children listen to this explanation and decide in their often pragmatic way that there is no Santa Claus, Easter Bunny, and Tooth Fairy, and that the spiritual business is just grown-up talk. This childhood experience may lay the foundation for our wondering if all belief in something or someone that we cannot see may, as we grow up, turn out to be mistaken, childish, foolish.

I am not trying to discourage parents from perpetuating the delightful myths of childhood. Far from it, partially because, in a society where other children believe in Santa Claus, the Easter Bunny, and the Tooth Fairy, the child who is different, who is the one who "knows better" than to believe in such things, is set apart from his friends at just the time when he should be learning to feel part of a group and interact well within it. The transition point for the child is very important to the whole matter of belief in later years, and yet it is difficult for parents to know if they are handling it successfully.

The experience of two sets of parents, similar in generation and outlook, will illustrate the haphazard nature of the transition. The daughters of both sets of parents were of above normal intelligence, but not exceptional. They both began to suspect that there was no flesh and blood Santa Claus at about the same age. And I think they both were told that Santa Claus was a spirit, the spirit of loving and giving. I know that the second child was so told, because I am she. The first child, however—let's call her Joanne—reacted with great pride that she had discovered that Santa Claus was what she considered a fraud, and she went about enthusiastically spreading the news to her little friends, some of whom were still midpoint in their discovery. She thought herself very clever. How do I know this about Joanne? I know it because now, as a grown woman, she still tells about how young she was when she made the discovery, apparently as a proof of her intelligence. No one could pull the wool over *her* eyes for very long. Joanne has maintained her blind cleverness into adulthood, being too sophisticated to believe in any God, much less the "stuff" about Jesus Christ. She seems to have no spiritual awareness at all. She has the same yearning to be loved that we all have, but it does not form a significant part of her thinking. What you see and touch and smell and hear and measure—that's all there is. To her, the rest of us are believing in fairies, whistling in the dark, partaking of the opium of the masses, living in the middle ages.

I remember being told the "truth" about Santa Claus in response to the specific questions that are normal for young children to ask. I also remember understanding what my parents meant about his being the spirit of giving. Without making too much of my experience from this many years away or overlaying it with complex theories, I can truthfully say that I distinctly remember the sense that something was "opening up," a new and adult way of understanding my world. In other words, the discovery about Santa Claus was an important step forward, as it was distinctly *not* for Joanne.

My point is that the idea of belief, when used in religion, can and often does work against our spiritual awareness. Belief is our mind's formulation of what we have received from life, including what we have been taught and what we ourselves have experienced. If, like Joanne, we have firmly disavowed belief in God, a spiritual force, or whatever, we are of course not likely to experience anything associated with what we don't believe exists. If we do say we believe, but if we honestly consider the evidence skimpy, we struggle and our belief is always open to the possibility that we will receive new evidence that will turn it into unbelief. Or we may try to force ourselves to believe, which is an exercise in futility if there ever was one! Going one step further, if we are firmly wedded to our stated beliefs, if they form an important part of who we consider we are, they can stand in the way of our receiving new input from our lives, because we will try to filter all experiences through them. We will not be open to the nuances of daily living, which is where God, or the Spirit, meets us.

So what if anything does theology, an intellectual system of affirmations concerning God, add to life? That many find it unnecessary, confusing, and indeed off-putting is one of my reasons for writing this book. The fact, however, is that some of us are so made that we want to analyze and explain our experience of life. Our minds jump to the task and never really let go of it completely. This is harmless and can be useful, as long as we recognize and remember that theology "is not where it's at." Living with compassion *is.*

A central Christian concept that seems to be a real stickler for many people is the idea of the Trinity. I have heard many Christians remark on it, saying, "How many gods are there anyway? I believe in *one* God. What is all this about three gods, all stuffed together into this Trinity idea?" I will not go into the history of the concept, which can be found elsewhere. The confusion it causes nowadays is evidence that it has outworn much of its usefulness. Nevertheless, I find it singularly appealing as long as it is not pushed too far.

Simply put, the concept of the Trinity is a way of expressing our awareness that the creator of the universe, the man Jesus, and the spirit of love as we experience it in our daily lives somehow share an identity. We recognize them as the same in essence. The Trinity *explains* nothing—it describes. It only affirms that the Spirit (the Ground of our Being, the Mystery, God) is strongly present in all three, and terms them the Creator, the Christ, and the Holy Spirit. No how or why. Alternate terms, "Father, Son, and Holy Ghost," only make matters worse by the archaic nature of their concepts. However, there is no need to throw out the baby with the bath water. The Trinity is an easy way of saying that yes, there is one God whom we experience in three different ways—as creator and sustainer of the universe, as an over-whelming presence in the man Jesus, and as an experience in our own little lives. Note that it doesn't rule out God's strong presence in another person, as for instance the Buddha, nor does it preclude other evidences of God.

This brief explanation of the Trinity is included here not only because I personally find it intellectually useful, but also because for many people it epitomizes the vagaries of theology, second only to the angel-on-the-head-of-a-pin argument. Most doctrines, no matter how odd they may seem to us now, derived from real religious experiences, although of another time. They are not foolishness. But neither are they necessary. The Spirit can be experienced whether or not we find theology helpful.

Whatever kind of person we are, we should be careful to keep all our thoughts about God, all our intellectual religious conclusions or semi-conclusions, in a state of flux as much as we can, basing our living on our past and immediate experience of life. This is a strong statement for me personally, having enjoyed delving into theology from my teen years on. I liked the intellectual challenge of fashioning a reasonable, coherent scheme about God and life, and so for a very long time I have been browsing in theological books, partly out of curiosity and partly hoping to find some new kernel of truth to reinvigorate my spiritual life. This is fine and good for those of us so made. The danger is that at some point we will say, "Okay, I now know all I need to know about God." And forget that knowing about God in general is not the same as meeting him here and now and trying to do this next moment, this coming day, what the Spirit would have us do.

I bumped into a new biblical source for this approach when I was church-hopping recently. Although I am a member of one particular congregation and usually attend its worship services, I sometimes wonder about other churches and ministers, so some Sundays I go visiting. Somewhat to my surprise, the minister of the church I had chosen to visit dropped a little gem in my lap, which I will tell about here, because it was new to me and may also be so to you. In a scanning of the Ten Commandments, he drew attention to the end of the first, "You shall not make yourself a graven image." In literal, historical context, the first commandment meant that the Israelites should not start following one of the many other gods being worshipped by other tribes and should not make any stone statues of their one God. The minister suggested that our firm ideas about what God is and does are also a type of graven image, and as such may block our meeting him and learning about him in our own lives. Point well taken, I thought. I was glad I had gone on my little excursion to another congregation that day.

During still another excursion, this time into a recent theological book, I came upon a full-length discussion of the same general topic of how the idea that we must "believe" this or that can hinder our encounter with the living God. Marcus Borg, in a splendid little book entitled *Meeting Jesus Again for the First Time*, writes of the problem he once had in trying to make Christian theology meaningful to himself, even to the point of questioning the reality of God. He traces his memories from childhood through seminary. Finally, in his mid-thirties, he had mystical moments of experiencing God completely apart from any belief about God. He writes that he began to understand that "the word *God* refers to the sacred at the center of existence, the holy mystery that is all around us and within us." [Borg, *Jesus*, 14] After studying about such experiences, he realized that they have occurred in all cultures and times and continue to do so, although they may still be considered extraordinary. He finally understood that God was real, a part of experience, not just a concept.

Much of Borg's book is devoted to describing how people since Jesus's time have tried to make logical sense of their experiences of God and in so doing developed theories—theologies—that to their minds, at the time and in the culture they were living, explained their experiences. (I like Hart's descriptions of theology as "the attempt to map ultimate reality." [Hart, 59]) Borg discusses three "macro-stories of scripture" that I think can help the modern reader to make existential sense of much of the Scriptures as well as consequent theologies. [Borg, 122-33] One of the "macro-stories" is the "exodus story" about bondage, liberation, journey, and destination; another is the "story of exile and return," about estrangement, alienation, and homecoming; and the third is the "priestly story" of sin, guilt, sacrifice, forgiveness, and acceptance. The first images the religious life as a journey from the life of bondage (to whatever) into a life of freedom from that bondage. The second deals with a sense of estrangement in the world that can become a journey of vital return to God. The third shows us as sinners in need of forgiveness and sacrifice. The theologies deriving from these stories are no longer automatically meaningful to most of us. They seem—and are—foreign, both in time and place, although with study we can understand their relevance.

At the very end of his book, Borg specifically discusses the word "believe," trying to return to its original definition, which over the years has been displaced by the shallower meaning of intellectually accepting the existence of something. He points out that it derives from both Greek and Latin words for "to give one's heart to." [Borg, *Jesus,* 137] He redefines it closer to its origins, writing that it "does not consist of giving one's mental assent to something, but involves a much deeper level of one's self." [Borg, *Jesus,* 137] It is a matter of being in a relationship to God that is all-important. It is a matter of trusting so completely in God's love and power that we will do what we know he would have us do. In other words, it is what we now generally call "faith."

But what about all the references to believing within the Bible? What do they mean? Interestingly, the Old Testament uses the word "believe" only four times. The first refers to believing that what Moses says is true, the second has as its object the ability of God to bring the Israelites out of the wilderness, and the remaining two similarly mean trust in God's ability, not his existence. Apparently there was little doubt about God's existence; the problem was whether he could and would save his chosen people. In the New Testament, however, belief in Jesus as the Christ is emphasized as a primary requirement. With few possible exceptions, the word is used in the sense of Borg's definition—giving one's heart to God, or in other terms, dedicating one's life to God. The existence of God, however, again is assumed.

Borg's redefinition makes the word less misleading, but meanwhile we are stuck with its current usage as intellectual assent to something that may be doubtful. So what word might we substitute in our talk and discussions? Instead of saying, "I believe in God," might we say "I am aware of the active power of a personal, creative Spirit"? How awk- ward, but the sentence does say what I and many others mean when we recite the creed. Instead of saying, "I believe in Jesus Christ, His only Son, our Lord," I actually mean, "I am aware of God's love and com- passion as it was perfectly exemplified in the Spirit of the historical per- son of Jesus." Even more awkward.

The solution my lie in three directions. Of course we cannot really erase the word "belief" from the language of religion, if for no other reason than that it occurs throughout the many translations of the New Testament, but we can try to avoid its current misuse. First, we can be careful and persistent in redefining the word in terms of its orig- inal meaning in our sermons and discussions. Second, I think we should avoid the word "belief" as much as we can, because it cannot but carry with it the aura of intellectual uncertainty. Often we can sub- stitute the word "faith," if what we mean is trust. A third and perhaps the most effective solution might be quietly to assume the existence of

theology— "belief/faith seeking understanding"
(from systematics class
    at seminary)   BELIEF and FAITH   21

the Spirit in our speech, much as God was an assumed entity for the people of the Bible.

Why need we talk of belief at all? The experience of God's Spirit is highly personal, marred and distorted rather than enhanced by description and discussion. We can decide simply not to talk in terms of what we believe or don't believe. Instead, we can try to reflect the activity of God's Spirit within our daily lives. Those who are aware of the Spirit will understand, and those still unaware will not be put off and separated from us as "believers" in some fairy tale. Or we can use the word "faith," not a synonym for "belief." Faith in someone is trust, without there being any question of the existence of that someone. Borg describes it as "the human response to God" [Borg, *God*, 168] and "the giving of one's heart, of one's self at its deepest level, to God. Its opposite is not doubt but infidelity." [Borg, *God*, 169] When we say that we have faith in God, we are not dealing with any question of his existence but expressing our trust in him. Winifred Gallagher, a behavioral scientist, after a search that led her through one religious group after another, said much the same thing: "St. Anselm said that he didn't seek to understand so that he could believe, but to believe so that he could understand. I've come to agree with the medieval philosopher, although I'd substitute 'trust' for 'believe'." [W. Gallagher, 316]

Whatever words we decide to use or not use, whatever theology we choose to embrace or eschew, we need to remember that our hearts, not our minds, are "where it's at," that we meet the Spirit in our daily living, not in our intellectual exercises, no matter how intriguing and stimulating—and even at times revealing—they may be.

vs. Barth's "The Wholly Other"?

◆   ◆   ◆

We also need to realize and remember that our meeting with the Spirit, like our meetings with other persons, is individual to us, although it may share many characteristics with the experiences of others. This diversity in spiritual experiences is the subject of the next chapter.

DISCUSSION QUESTIONS

How did learning "the truth" about Santa Claus affect you?

How important is it to you to reason about God and the meaning of life?

Is the concept of the Trinity meaningful to you?

Do you keep your ideas about God in flux?

Are any of the three "macro-stories" meaningful to you? Do you feel (1) in bondage and needing to be freed, (2) estranged and needing to feel at home in the world, or (3) sinful and needing to be forgiven?

3

DIVERSITY and SPIRITUAL EXPERIENCE

If grace perfects nature it must expand all our natures into the full richness of the diversity which God intended when He made them, and Heaven will display far more variety than Hell. [C. S. Lewis, *Prayer*, 10]

Too often we wish for certainty, particularly in the spiritual realm. We want to know for sure that there is an all-powerful God who cares about us. And furthermore we want to be told by that God exactly what we should do to live a happy life, today, tomorrow, and always. In effect, we are yearning to return to and remain in childhood, real or idealized, where parents who loved us always told us clearly and exactly what behavior they expected from us.

Certainty is indeed offered by various religious groups, which is—along with their promise of a caring family situation—a primary source of their attraction. Absolute conviction is also expressed by individuals, at times much to the consternation of their less convinced acquaintances. An example of this occurred years ago, when I was participating in a discussion group for adult members of a suburban church. Among us was one young woman, Margaret, who was more up front than the rest of us about the fact that she was searching for something, that she felt that her present life was lacking the spirituality that she yearned for. Margaret was a very pretty mother of three children, married to a man who was not interested in "deep" discussions. Brought up in this same area and in this same church, she was its volunteer of volunteers. Whenever there was a job needing to be done that no one else wanted to do, Margaret would offer to do it, and she always did it well. She was what one would consider an exemplary Christian and church member. And yet she felt herself seriously lacking spiritually.

Steve, on the other hand, did not feel himself spiritually lacking at all. He was a born-again Christian, and he had "Jesus in his heart." As a young man, Steve had indulged in drugs, had abused his first wife, and all in all had led what he termed a "dissolute life." Then had come his conversion, the time that he "had let Jesus into his heart." Since then, everything had come up roses. He was changed, not perfect yet, but working at it with the help of his Lord and his Bible, every word of which he maintained was literal fact. Margaret listened with rapt attention. Although she did not say, "This is what I want. How can I get it?," she made it obvious time and again that this was what she was feeling.

And what did the rest of us do? Did we ask Steve what he meant by having "Jesus in his heart"? No, we did not, because as Christians we felt that perhaps we should already know ourselves what he meant, and we certainly weren't going to let everyone else know that we did not have Jesus in our hearts. What we did, as a group, was question the literalness of Steve's approach to the Bible. There were numerous polite and careful skirmishes between Steve and the rest of us. At first, he was out to convert us all to his interpretation of the Bible, but later, clearly failing in his attempt, he apparently felt odd man out and uncomfortable. After four or five sessions, he just didn't show up any more.

I had been disturbed about Margaret's obvious longing for Steve's certainty. I made an abortive attempt to say something about how we all experience God differently, but she paid absolutely no attention to me. Her eyes were on Steve. He had a certainty that she wanted, and she was hoping somehow to find out the secret of getting it. I don't know how Margaret has fared in her spiritual quest, because I moved from the area. But I will always remember her lovely face, chin upturned, watching Steve and yearning to be like him, certain in belief and God's expectations.

As I see it now, Margaret's dilemma was that she wanted to experience the Spirit of God exactly as Steve did, rather than in her own way, but she didn't even know how to begin. Attracted by his certainty, she didn't understand that the Spirit comes to each of us differently, filtered by who we are. I strongly doubt that Margaret would ever know what Steve meant by having "Jesus in his heart." I don't know either—although I can sort of guess—because I am not Steve nor similar to him in most ways.

Paul in 1 Corinthians 12:4 puts it this way: "Now there are diversities of gifts, but the same Spirit." Many ministers interpret this scripture narrowly, although appropriately, in terms of a Christian congregation, pointing out that within the congregation we have different but equally important functions. But the scripture carries a broader message. It is reminding us that people are very diverse, and therefore that the Spirit we receive from God will be experienced and evidenced differently, but that it is nevertheless the same Spirit. It is like one light going through different pieces of colored glass, some green, some blue, some red—but the same light.

One cannot discuss differences in spiritual experience without referring to William James, whose *The Varieties of Religious Experience* is as relevant and comprehensive today as it was in 1902, when it was written. As did many, I first read this gem of a book in my college years and felt much enlightened. Rereading it in preparation for writing this book, I felt not enlightenment, since I had already had that on my first reading, but discouragement. James convincingly sets forth so much that has been totally ignored or forgotten, despite numerous restatements by others over the years. His message has not reached the multitude—whoever they are—who still confuse facts with the meaning of those facts. An example of such confusion is the idea that if the universe was created over a long period of time rather than in the biblical one week (the fact), then there was no Spirit behind the creation (the meaning). In James's work, the distinction is made as preparation for describing extreme accounts of religious experiences without passing judgment as to their value.

For us, the important conclusion reached by James after examining in great detail all sorts of religious experiences, some quite far out, is that our experiences are as different as our personalities, and that we should each be both satisfied with our own and also tolerant of the other person's. He puts it this way:

> ...I do not see how it is possible that creatures in such different positions and with such different powers as human individuals are, should have exactly the same functions and the same duties. No two of us have identical difficulties, nor should we be expected to work out identical solutions. Each, from his peculiar angle of observation, takes in a certain sphere of fact and trouble, which each must deal with in a unique manner.... Unquestionably, some men have the more complete experience and the higher vocation, here just as in the social world; but for each man to stay in his own experience, whate'er it be, and for others to tolerate him there, is surely best." [James, 378-79]

Tolerance of diversity is much encouraged these days, and rightly so. Less emphasized is what James refers to as "stay[ing] in [one's] own experience." Margaret's problem lay exactly there, in her inability to accept who she was and recognize that she could not experience the Spirit in any way but her own, certainly not in Steve's way.

The Bible, like many other spiritual writings, is so full of such a variety of wise observations and advice that we may miss what is most relevant to us personally and concentrate on parts that do not increase our spiritual awareness. Someone like Margaret may concentrate on New Testament scriptures that seem to indicate that there is no other way to God than through Jesus, when what she needs are passages about the nearness and presence of God, both before and after Jesus's life. Two come immediately to mind, but there are many others. In Psalm 139, the author asks, "Whither shall I go from thy Spirit? Or whither shall I flee from thy presence?" (vs. 7) The other is the striking statement of this theme in Paul's letter to the Romans: "For I am sure that neither death, nor life, nor angels, nor principalities, nor things present, nor things to come, nor power, nor height, nor depth, nor anything else in all creation, will be able to separate us from the love of God in Christ Jesus our Lord." (Romans 8:38-39)

Margaret was like a little old lady looking for her glasses when they were right there, pushed back up on her head. The point is the disarmingly simple one, admittedly sometimes hard to realize and accept, that God is right here, right now, with you and with me. As I sit at the computer, he is not somewhere up there in the sky, or waiting outside for me to remember him as I survey a beautiful meadow, or even floating above my bed awaiting my night prayers. He is here, "in my face," as the expression goes. God is meeting me in the life I am living, here and now, whether my mind is on him or not. In the same way he is meeting you, as you sit quietly reading these words. In a sense, no big deal, because he has always been there right with you your entire life as you have been meeting each moment. This second is no different from any other. In another sense, of course, there has never been a "bigger deal." Contemplating God's presence has understandably frightened men from the beginning of time. My next chapter, The Eternal Now and Daily Life, discusses possible ways to realize God's presence more fully.

Another part of our experience of the Mystery, the Spirit, is the sense of God as deep, deep within us, acting within and through our conscience and our subconscious. Differently in each of us, reflecting our uniqueness. Hart writes that "deep inside us, well below the surface of our ordinary consciousness and usual mental activity is a place incredibly still, like a small chapel. Here is another locus of the encounter, at the core of our being." [Hart, 28] It is to this aspect of God that we appeal when we have difficult or major decisions to make that are not clearly decided by love of our neighbor. For example, the young adult who wants to "do God's will" is about to decide upon a career. Should every young adult decide to become a missionary in India or live with and help the sick and helpless? Some sense within their deepest selves a yearning and an ability to follow one of those courses. Most of us do not. Mother Theresa herself was very vocal about saying that loving and obeying God does not mean going off to a foreign country to help the sick, as she felt called to do, but rather loving and helping the person near to you in your daily life. Another decisionmaking time occurs for the older adult upon retirement. Volunteering for a social service program is an obvious way to go, but which one? To help the poor, the elderly, the young, and on and on. Or perhaps some other course.

We often forget how different we are, that God created each of us as unique persons, like the proverbial snowflake, and as the creator of our individual life he wants us, as we develop, to fulfill the possibilities of our genes. Think of the myriad upon myriad of possibilities in each human mating: that particular ovum descending at that time rather than another, and then the unbelievable number of individual sperms, with just the one that makes it inside to join with that particular ovum and become the beginning of one new person—you. Having created this particular life, God intends it to blossom fully, to become what it and it alone should be—not what another individual should be. God is within us, helping the bud to open in its own way, to reveal each of us for what we were born to be and become.

So what are we to do when we face a major decision? There are no rules to follow, much as we might wish there were. No certainties. We may read words of wisdom, and we may consult close friends and advisors, but the answer ultimately must come from far down inside us where we and only we can find it. Only we can know who we really are and can be. The decision is ours. It is to be "found within our own deepest wanting," as Thomas Hart puts it. [Hart, 138] We must remember that God is not against us in any way, not on "the other side," wanting us to do what we don't want to do, a concept that has been widely assumed in Western culture. Hart declares succinctly that "the moral of the entire biblical story is that God wants life for us. The divine purpose could hardly be clearer." [Hart, 125] Writing of the "deepest wanting," he notes that "Carl Jung frequently urges this same basic idea, though in a different conceptual framework. He stresses the importance of following our destiny, which he says flows out of our inner being.... The seeds of our destiny, or God's purpose for us, are planted within us." [Hart, 140]

At major decision points, this means that our prayer for help must be directed inside, we must search ourselves for what it is that we do most deeply want. Time may elapse as we do this, because we may not, when we are very young, have yet developed a knowledge of who we are, what our possibilities are, what we really want to do. Most of us who have become aware of the world of the Spirit would like to feel "called" to something that is clearly God's will. However, although we are all called—created—to be compassionate toward our neighbor, we are not all called to teach Sunday School or work among the poor. Some are called to work with computers—they have immediate aptitude and are fascinated by the complexity and possibilities of electronic communication. Others are called to compose or perform music—obviously talented and captivated by the expressiveness of sounds. Still others are called, at least early in their lives, to mate and nurture children, with other important desires not fully developed and recognizable.

This principle of relying on "our own deepest wanting," Hart reminds us, "has just one presupposition: that one's life is generally oriented toward God." [Hart, 138] A completely materialistic person, who has not yet discovered the truth of the old saw that "money cannot buy happiness," may look inside himself and find only a desire to accumulate money so he can feel superior to the other guy. Someone else may gleefully discover his persuasiveness with groups of people and realize that *power* can be his, power over other people and glory for himself. So develops a Hitler. In other words, the presupposition of wanting to do God's will is important.

Often we need patience. We look deep inside and discover many diverse aptitudes and interests, but no keen "wanting." Then we must wait until such a "wanting" develops, perhaps for years. For me personally, there have been three such strong desires, none aimed clearly and precisely at helping others. Having been spiritually aware and raised within a religion, I found this disturbing. Had God no purpose for me? It didn't occur to me that becoming fully *me* might in itself be a purpose. That God really, honestly, cherished me as an individual never entered my mind, and if it had, I would have thought I was in danger of becoming horribly self-centered and conceited. So were many of us raised.

The first wanting was certainly ordinary. I wanted to marry a particular man and then to have his children. I desired this strongly enough so that, when my husband and I were told that our chance of becoming parents was miniscule, I pushed hard to adopt a baby and we did. Three natural children followed, slowly but surely, and I dedicated myself enthusiastically and joyfully to nurturing my brood. Then, just as my little ones were almost completely fledged, I discovered the beauty and thrill of horses in a big way. They became my passion. I started riding and jumping lessons, I became expert enough to fox hunt with enthusiasm and (relative) safety, and eventually I owned two horses and spent every weekend riding the trails with friends. Did I consider this activity in line with God's will for me? Never entered my head in that way. But my passion for horses is surely a part of who I am, and I still own and care for two horses and ride out with friends whenever the weather permits. Only recently have I realized that this is okay, this is not selfishness. Horses do not consume my entire life, but if they were to disappear there would be a large emptiness.

My third, and perhaps final—but who knows?—deep wanting is to write, as I am now obviously doing. All my books have been, in one form or another, attempts to share with others the wisdom that I have been gaining over the years. My desire to write about what I have learned had been slowly appearing while I was spending twenty-five years earning my living as a salaried writer. Only after retirement did it start to feel essential to my life.

I have never let either writing or horses interfere with the three full days I spend in volunteer work with the elderly. I have firmly set compassionate action in first place, because in this I know intellectually that I am doing God's will and I can see clearly that I am making others happier. As for my books, I can only hope that they will reach others who will find them helpful in their daily lives. And perhaps the relegation of writing to second place has helped retain its appeal for me.

Which leads to another important point: success is not guaranteed. We may feel a deep wanting to do something, recognize that this is what we were "meant" to do, and proceed to do it as well as we can, whether it be working with computers, performing music, or raising children, and lo and behold—after all that—we do not become the inventor of a new piece of software, we develop into second-rate violinists, and our children become involved with drugs or worse. We are disappointed, but we are wrong if we think that following our deepest desires was a mistake. The world needs computer programmers who work with others' software; second-rate violinists still play beautiful music; and perhaps our work with our children will show up later in their lives. For years I kept a saying by Mother Theresa on my mirror that made the point that following what we knew was God's will was not a guarantee of success in our endeavors.

At the end of our life, we may look back and realize that the big mistake may have been *not* to have followed our deepest wanting. We may have thought that it didn't sound virtuous enough, or perhaps we listened to the advice of our father and took up the career he wanted us to have instead of the one our heart desired. It all comes down to recognizing that we are indeed unique, we are not the other guy, and God wants us to discover who we are and then go with it.

Back to Margaret, who is still in my mind's eye, looking so hard at Steve as if by looking she could somehow capture the mystical quality of his experience of "Jesus in his heart" and the certainty of his conviction that everything he needed to know was in the Bible. She was seeking God, not knowing, as Martin Buber put it, that "there is no such thing as seeking God, for there is nothing in which He [can] not be found." [Buber, 80] How could one help her to become conscious of God's presence and of her own uniqueness in his sight? For those are the two sticking points. Consciousness of God's Spirit is a major part of being spiritually alive.

One yearns to say, "But Margaret, he is there, with you, in you. You are already receiving and reflecting him in your own unique way, in the Margaret way of kindness, service, and faithfulness. Forget any intellectual problems, ignore any desire for mystical experience. He is with you in the special form in which you are made to receive him. Relax, rejoice, and be thankful." And I guess I am now saying exactly that to any Margaret who may be reading what I write, hoping that this time she will hear and say, quite simply, "Yes, of course," and go about her daily business of spreading love and discovering her special place in the world.

◆　　　◆　　　◆

This experience that I wish for all Margarets, of knowing in their own way that God is with them, here and now, is the subject of the next chapter.

DISCUSSION QUESTIONS

Have you ever known anyone like either Margaret or Steve?

How would you ideally like to experience God? How would you like him to "speak" to you?

How would you—again ideally—like to serve God? Might this be more for human praise than service?

Have you made choices in your life that respond to a "deepest wanting?"

4

THE ETERNAL NOW and DAILY LIFE

> We may ignore, but we can nowhere evade, the presence of God. The world is crowded with Him. He walks everywhere *incognito*. And the *incognito* is not always hard to penetrate. The real labour is to remember, to attend. In fact, to come awake. Still more, to remain awake. [Lewis, *Prayer,* 75]

I have always admired the phrase "the Eternal Now" for both its message and its brevity. It takes two time-related and apparently contradictory words and crushes them together. The first is a symbol for either the intellectual concept of unending time or—more to the point—the spiritual concept of timelessness, while the other is a symbol for their exact opposite, the split second of the physically experienced moment even as we say the word. The result is that, if the phrase has meaning, it presents a paradox—a circumstance that appears with such disconcerting regularity in a search for truth that it almost seems to confirm it.

The phrase, as I first encountered it years ago, occurred in *Behold the Spirit* by Alan Watts, an Anglican priest at the time of writing (1947) and later an exponent of Zen Buddhism. He writes of the Eternal Now as the "here-and-now-ness" of our encounter with God. (Watts uses the term "union" with God, but having read Martin Buber on the I-Thou relationship of man to God, I realize that "union" tends to obliterate the otherness of the almighty God and to feel a bit unrealistically "cozy"—my term, not that of the more dignified and poetic Buber!)

35

Watts's book phrases and rephrases the central idea of the present-ness of God at every moment in our lives: "What we have to realize, therefore, is not the getting of union with God, but the not being able to get away from it. It is in, it *is* this Eternal Now, wherein God so lovingly holds us." [Watts, 100] The same thought is amplified: "God is the most obvious thing in the world, the most self-evident, and union with God is the primary and most unavoidable reality of our lives. Yet God is so obvious and so unavoidable and so close to us that we are not aware of him. To try to see God is like trying to look at your own eyes, for he is nearer to us than we are to ourselves." [Watts, 26] The New Testament abounds in affirmations of God's continual presence in our lives, as does the Old Testament. The most familiar, in Psalm 139 and Romans 8, were quoted in the last chapter. Pierre Teilhard de Chardin, the French Jesuit paleontologist and philosopher, writing in the early twentieth century, put it this way: "By means of all created things, without exception, the divine assails us, penetrates us, and molds us. We imagine it as distant and inaccessible, whereas in fact we live steeped in its burning layers." [quoted by Annie Dillard, 87] And certainly the literature of religions outside the Judeo-Christian tradition provides similar descriptions of God's omnipresence and availability.

A danger in emphasizing the nearness of God is that we will forget that he is also very much the Other, the Creator, the Judge, big and fearful and so far beyond us puny human beings that we can barely comprehend him. This is the God of Job. Cynthia Ozick, in her essay entitled *The Impious Impatience of Job*, writes vividly of God's response to Job's questioning of him: "God's answer, a fiery challenge, roils out of the whirlwind. 'Where were *you*,' the Almighty roars, in supernal strophes that blaze through the millennia, 'when I laid the foundation of the earth?' And what comes crashing and tumbling out of the gale is an exuberant ode to the grandeur of the elements..." [Ozick, 210] Aware of the mighty Mystery of the universe, it is no wonder that we have difficulty realizing that God is also within each one of us, the "still small voice of calm," the indwelling Spirit. In other words, he is both way out there and also way deep down inside us. C. S. Lewis writes that we ought to be "simultaneously aware of closest proximity and infinite distance." [Lewis, *Prayer,* 13] Hart speaks of God as "at the edges of our awareness." [Hart, 27] We may visualize the Spirit as a lens through which we meet life.

We must not, however, neglect a very basic element in our experience of the Eternal Now, of the Spirit—movement. The word "spirit" is derived from the Latin word for "breath." The dictionary has a long column replete with ways the word is used, most having to do with motion, vigor, and personality. Even a spirit, used in the ghostly sense, is *someone,* the remains or essence of a person, not of a thing and not thin air. The commonest metaphor for the Spirit or God—and to my mind the best—is that of wind, similar to breath, of course, but importantly emanating from the outside, not from the human mouth. In John 3:8, Jesus himself compares the Spirit of God to a wind: "The wind blows where it wills, and you hear the sound of it, but you do not know whence it comes or whither it goes; so it is with every one who is born of the Spirit." And in the description of Pentecost in the beginning of Acts, Luke writes: "When the day of Pentecost had come, they were all together in one place. And suddenly a sound came from heaven like the rush of a mighty wind, and it filled all the house where they were sitting.... And they were all filled with the Holy Spirit..." [Acts 2:1-4]

The important question, of course, is what does the Eternal Now mean for us, for you and me, very much living in the here and now? Well and good to say that God is always present and that experiencing the Eternal Now is wonderful indeed, but how are we to discover that experience? We have not changed from those people about whom Alan Watts wrote in 1947:

> Today, in Church and out of Church, there are thousands of souls
> who realize in varying degrees of clarity that what they want from
> religion is not a collection of doctrinal and ritual symbols, nor a
> series of moral precepts. They want God Himself, by whatever

name he may be called; they want to be filled with his creative life
and power; they want some conscious experience of being at one
with Reality itself, so that their otherwise meaningless and ephem-
eral lives may acquire an eternal significance." [Watts, 24]

So let us turn to a description of the three stages that usually precede
awareness of the Eternal Now and then the three circumstances under
which it sometimes happens. Stage one on the way to the Eternal Now
experience is becoming conscious of a need for something besides food,
shelter, money, sex, power, and companionship. Books and magazine
articles have been announcing our culture's hunger for spiritual food as
long as I can remember, but perhaps with increasing frequency in the
last several years. I can assume that anyone who has picked up this
book already is conscious of this need, so I won't elaborate on the
point.

Stage two happens as we become aware that there really is the possibility for fulfilling this need, that there is a spiritual world, a deeper
reality beneath "everyday reality" that provides meaning for us as individuals. The awareness seems to occur either in a sudden flash of realization like those discussed in my next chapter, Epiphanies and
Memory, or in a gradual perception that the most valuable thing that
life has to offer, and without which life eventually tastes like dust and
ashes, is the affection and love experienced in encounters with other
people. This perception then leads to realizing that love and affection
somehow belong to a different order from our everyday superficial
comings and goings, gettings and spendings, and other laying waste of
our powers (to paraphrase the familiar Wordsworth lines).

We move ourselves into stage three when, becoming more aware of
the spiritual level of life, we decide to focus on it enough to realize and
intellectually acknowledge that there is indeed a single and recognizable Spirit underlying our life. We sense that it can make our life
meaningful and even joyful. We intuitively know that it has to do with
love and compassion toward other people, that natural beauty is somehow a part of it, and that it seems first to overwhelm us with its reality

and then to disappear so completely that we almost—almost—forget that we ever knew it. We recognize it, we want to experience and flow with it, but although we try, we find that we cannot grasp it or join it.

At this point, we would be wise to remember the images that others have used to describe the Spirit. It is like air, all around us, necessary to sustain human life but invisible. We only notice it when it moves, becoming a breeze or a wind, but it is there all the time and it can be immensely powerful. The Spirit is also likened to running water, necessary to life, not to be grasped without destroying its nature, but beautiful and at times overwhelming. Both air and water abound, they are essential to life, but they are not tame. Although we domesticate them in many ways for our use, the occasional disastrous occurrence of hurricanes, floods, and tornadoes reminds us that air and water remain unconquered substances. My point is that gentleness and availability can be, and are, in our daily experience, combined with the possibility for tremendous power. It should therefore not be a foreign idea to us that the Spirit, whom we experience most often in an everyday setting in a gentle fashion, as love, compassion, and healing, can also be the creator of the universe itself.

If we intellectually accept the notion of a deeper reality sustaining our ordinary life, and particularly if we have had even a brief (although perhaps at the time unrecognized) experience of the Spirit's presence, we want and indeed often yearn for more, realizing somehow that "that is where it's at." We wish to learn how to become aware of it more often, how to partake of its peace, joy, and even power. Watts says that we have the "freedom...to appreciate, affirm and realize" [Watts, 90] our encounter with God—or not to, of course. The question becomes, how does this awareness occur in us? Can we ourselves do anything to increase its frequency? Jesus in the New Testament answers this question repeatedly, saying that if we knock at the door—if we ask, if we strongly desire, if we in effect become alert—we will at last become aware of the presence of the Spirit in the moment, which then assumes the quality of eternity.

The precious realization of the Eternal Now (the presence at this moment of the Mystery, the Spirit, God, the Ground of Being) seems to me, from my own experience and from my reading, to come to us primarily, but not exclusively, under three circumstances. The first is when we notice something happening to us or in us. As with air becoming breeze, we sense motion of some sort. But how many breezes have we *not* noticed and appreciated, although we have certainly been present and awake? Those that we have especially noticed have come when we are hot and uncomfortable, looking for that movement of air that will bring relief and pleasure. Nevertheless, we know that if we had paid attention at other more comfortable moments, we might well have noticed that there was a breeze.

Examples of spiritual breezes abound. One is the especially warm affection we feel when our grandchild puts out her arms to us to be picked up. Another is the rush of concern when we see an injured bird. Still another is the distress we experience in watching sick and hungry refugees on a television screen. I have intentionally chosen small, daily incidents of our own love and compassion. When they occur, we would be wise to notice and to say, quite simply, "Yes, that's it. That is the Spirit, that is the wonderful, small breeze coming through me." Our language in fact reflects our sense that something from outside us leads to our compassion. Consider the phrase that someone "was moved" to do something.

The second circumstance that may make us aware of the Spirit is when it moves through other people and we are awake enough to notice and identify it. We don't ourselves feel the breeze, but we see it moving the grass over there in the field. We might simply notice the affection, concern, or distress of someone *else* picking up a grandchild, observing an injured bird, or watching refugees on television. More likely, however, we will observe the Spirit moving others in a caring way when it is toward us. Not every "good deed," however, is an example of the Spirit moving. If we are sick and our niece visits us, she may only be "doing her duty." After all, one *should* visit a sick aunt. The difference between duty and the movement of the Spirit may be seen in the eyes primarily, and then in the unconscious body language. When there is clear empathy, when our niece has made the effort to understand how we feel with her heart, when her emotions and not just her mind are touched by our plight, we can sense a sort of movement of her toward us. That is not overstatement, as you will realize if you remember to analyze such an incident as it happens, or perhaps even in memory. Again, we can say, "There it is, that's it, that is the Spirit moving."

The third circumstance in which we may experience the Eternal Now is probably what makes it most valuable to us and lures us into watching for it. The Spirit not only passes through us as we extend our love to others, but—being a spirit of love—it also somehow and sometimes makes us know that we *ourselves* are loved, that we are cherished by that incredibly loving and powerful spirit. It is this awareness that allows us to forget about our little egos and to pass on its love to others. We sense ourselves somehow in step with the universe, going with the stream, partaking of its power. We feel not only that we are cherished but that our lives have meaning.

I could here summarize what men and women throughout the ages have written to explain *why* awareness of God—the Eternal Now—brings with it the knowledge of being cherished by the creator, the ability to love our fellowman, and the sense of power that comes with being allied with the Spirit, but all that is secondary. If our intellects wish to build a theology based on our experience, we can certainly do so and join the thousands of others who have come up with explanations of their experience of the Eternal Now, the Spirit, God, the Mystery.

But what matters is not the theology but coming to the experience more often. And what can we ourselves do to make that happen? Really, very little, but that little is important. After the three stages have occurred leading to intellectual acknowledgement of the Spirit, of the Eternal Now, all we can do is watch for it and learn to recognize it in the circumstances in which we know that it may come—when we ourselves sense a spirit of love toward another, when someone else shows that spirit of love to us or someone else, and when we come to know that we ourselves are treasured by that same Spirit. The more we want it, the more we watch for it, and the more we expect it—not tomorrow, but today—really, right now, the more likely we will become aware of it. Then we can in a sense access it more easily. Jane Goodall writes that she tries "to keep a finger hooked into the spiritual power as it were." [Goodall, 268]

Meanwhile, we should be careful that we get ourselves out of the way, that we stop our struggling and theorizing. Watts says that we may "fail to see through the window because we are painting pictures on the glass." [Watts, 25] We understandably want to do something ourselves, to grasp after the experience. However, all we need to do is say, "Yes, the Spirit is indeed here, unavoidable, cherishing me and moving through me if I will let it." The clouds will not break open and there will be no thunder and lightening, but the world will look very different. And then, as you know or as I hope you will know, the feeling of thankfulness becomes almost overwhelming.

We live in a world permeated with the Eternal Now, a present moment supported by and infused with a spiritual reality. While we look out on our everyday, black-and-white, ordinary life asking, "Where is this Eternal Now? How do I meet it?" we are at the same moment in it and meeting it, or more accurately, it is meeting us. In fact, we cannot escape it. If we shut our eyes on the black-and-white world for a second, consider, and then open them in expectation, we may see that what we mistook for a world of black and white is in reality a world of color that has all along been underlying what we had thought was a colorless world. It is the world of the Eternal Now.

In this way we may know "the vital, lively nature of the Eternal Now [which] imparts a certain *joie de vivre* that expresses itself naturally and spontaneously like the song of a bird. It issues in a profound and joyous acceptance of the will of God as this is expressed in the circumstances of each moment, for we realize that all these are included in and governed by the Eternal Now, the love of God." [Watts, 108]

◆   ◆   ◆

The exceptional moments of realization, epiphanies, are the subject of the next chapter.

DISCUSSION QUESTIONS

Does the phrase "the Eternal Now" have meaning for you or do you find the paradox disturbing and not related to your daily life?

Do the three stages preceding awareness of the Eternal Now make psychological sense to you?

Do the three circumstances when an awareness of the Eternal Now is most likely to occur make psychological sense to you? Can you give personal examples? Can you give other examples of the Spirit moving, perhaps from your own experience?

5

EPIPHANY and MEMORY

> When we think certain states of mind superior to others, is it ever because of what we know concerning their organic antecedents? No! it is always for two entirely different reasons. It is either because we take an immediate delight in them; or else it is because we believe them to bring us good consequential fruits for life. [James, 31]

An epiphany is not forgotten. The word "epiphany" derives from the Greek for a "coming to light," a "manifestation," or an "appearance." I have always liked its sound and the cathedral-like ups and downs of its letters when handwritten. I first heard the word in its meaning as a season of the Christian church, celebrating the coming of the Wise Men twelve days after Christmas. I use the word here, however, in its definition as "a usually sudden perception of the nature or meaning of something" or "an intuitive grasp of reality usually through something simple and striking."

Most of us treasure such an experience to the point that we speak of it rarely, afraid to lessen its value by the diluting action of speech and repetition. We hold it close to us as a high point of our life. And so it is. I suspect that many of us, however, put it away carefully in our little jewel box, to look at now and again with pleasure, nostalgia, and perhaps awe. We may not realize that it provides a reliable basis, along with reason, for a deeper understanding of our world and may be the source of a power given in a unique form exclusively to us for daily use.

I suspect that we all have had at least one personal epiphany by the time we reach adulthood, whether we recognize it as such or not. In our skeptical and agnostic age, some people may try to ignore or dismiss such sudden perceptions as nonsense, aberrations of their subconscious, irrational experiences to be put behind them. Nevertheless, I suspect the epiphany is remembered, sunk though it may be into a deep, dark corner of the mind.

By epiphany, I mean the brief and powerful spiritual experience that may or may not be religious in nature, rather than the more frequent, everyday awareness of the spiritual element of life that many people know and that I discuss in other chapters. Epiphanies are at the heart of all religions, despite the different names and interpretations given them. They are also known by people who claim no religion. I think that most of us may have one or two in our jewel box even if we are agnostics, atheists, or "couldn't-care-less-about-religion" people.

I must again refer to psychologist William James and his *The Varieties of Religious Experience*. Based on lectures given at the University of Edinburgh, the book is—in James's own words—"loaded with concrete examples," of which he chose the most extreme manifestations of what he calls the "religious temperament." The book is indeed "loaded," to the point of tiring the conscientious reader who attempts to ingest them all. One closes the book very aware that people of all kinds have had powerful religious experiences that they have interpreted in as many ways as there were people.

James names four qualities that distinguish what we are here terming epiphanies and what he calls "mystical states." The first quality is "ineffability," meaning that they are very difficult to describe adequately. The second is a "noetic quality," indicating that they feel like a state of knowledge and "carry with them a curious sense of authority for aftertime." The third is "transiency," because they do not last long. And the last is "passivity," in that we experience them as an influx from beyond us and are unable to bring them about ourselves. He adds that "some memory of their content always remains, and a profound sense of their importance." [James, 299-301] The similarity among all religions and philosophies of the mystical state is significant. James writes that there is about mystical utterances an eternal unanimity which ought to make a critic stop and think.' [James, 329]

As I said above, James has deliberately presented the extremes of religious experience, some by people that we would call at the least "unbalanced." He points out, however, that similar experiences occur to many of us in daily life. He writes of "the simplest rudiment of mystical experience" as "that deepened sense of the significance of a maxim or formula which occasionally sweeps over one. 'I've heard that said all my life,' we exclaim, 'but I never realized its full meaning until now.'" [James, 301] James's example—which all of us must recognize—draws the sting of weirdness and otherworldliness that may repel us in the word "mysticism." It is, however, such a mild example of a spiritual experience that it just manages to sneak into the lowest level of my meaning of epiphany.

I continue with James for a moment because, out of the wealth of his research, he draws three conclusions about the "truth" of mystical experience for daily life. The first is that they are usually and "have the right to be" authoritative to the individual experiencing them, which means that they probably will and should affect the way he lives his life; the second is that they are not so nor should they be so to anyone else, which would eliminate proselytism and intolerance based on the experience; and the third is that they make us realize that the intellect and the senses are not our only ways to truth. James phrases the last by writing that they "break down the authority of the non-mystical or rationalistic consciousness, based upon the understanding and the sense alone.... They open out the possibility of other orders of truth." [James, 331] The importance to us here lies in the balance between what we believe and are taught to believe with our minds on the one hand and what we personally experience with our spirit on the other.

What might be initially seen as an anti-intellectual emphasis in this and other chapters—but is really simply an attempt to make our rational minds acknowledge and welcome spiritual experience as a reliable source of truth—is not a natural one for me. Brought up in a Lutheran church, I attended Sunday School as a child and then was a member of the class for young people being brought into the church as full members. The minister who taught it had his act together, and I quickly grasped the logic of the Christian beliefs and was delighted that it all made so much sense, given certain assumptions. A few years later, I found my older brother's philosophy textbook during the summer and had a great time comparing different systems. Spinoza in particular fascinated me. So inspired, I even wrote a piece on my own philosophy of life—probably highly eclectic—based on the idea that everyone wants to be happy. In college, I made certain to choose classes on the origins of the Bible, basic Christian theology, and philosophy. I attended a Lutheran church in Cambridge, Massachusetts, with a minister who again clearly had his intellectual act together and in addition was an inspiring preacher. I knew what I "believed" and that it made sense. However, this "belief" was built on other people's experiences and interpretations, not on my own. A certain "leap of faith" in the validity of the experiences of those other people was required. I hoped I had made that leap and certainly tried to keep on making it.

And then, toward the end of my sophomore year, I fell in love. At first, the experience was not religious although certainly cataclysmic—as apparently it is for most people. Color appears where previously there was only black and white. Our enemies become our friends, and our friends become our bosom buddies. Of course our beloved becomes perfect, as well as essential to our every moment. But my beloved was not there for my every moment, having graduated from law school and departed for a job in Washington, D.C. while I was still a junior in college. We were engaged to be married the next year and exchanged long, daily letters. It was while writing to him that my very first epiphany occurred, and it was a religious one. I recognized that the aura of love I felt for the whole world as a result of my love for a particular man was what God must feel for each person. I knew that this love, which clearly originated outside me, was the Spirit of God moving through me. The cause was God: the occasion was my being in love. I had the edifice of belief all ready, and here came the basement that could sustain it. And has sustained it ever since, as a matter of fact, with extra bricks and stone appearing now and then to provide an even stronger base for the building.

Following through on the imagery, I found that the arrival of my children, with the powerful and long-lasting love that came with each one, extended the basement considerably and made it strong enough to sustain extensions of the intellectual edifice gradually rising above it as the years brought more understanding of life.

Not all epiphanies are felt and interpreted as religious in nature, nor are all as strong and definitive to one's later life as those that I experienced as a young woman. And as William James discovered in his exhaustive research on religious experience, "these experiences can be as infinitely varied as are the idiosyncrasies of individuals." [James, 320] An older man responded to my question about epiphanies in his life by recounting his experience on Okinawa when he was stationed there over fifty years ago. He was relaxing with friends in a beautiful location, looking down over peaceful woods and fields, when he was momentarily filled with the knowledge that life could be beautiful, that all the fighting made no sense, and that people could and should live peaceably and simply together. Rather obvious, no? He too knew all this before, but in his epiphany he knew it differently and more forcibly. He combined this experience with his admiration for several of his servicemen buddies who had built a house for themselves using only materials that they had found in the area. Much later, after retirement, he himself built a house with his own hands, not however with found materials. His experience was spiritual in that it enforced his already gentle nature and life-altering in that it was part of what led him to build his own house, but it was certainly not religious nor even moral in the sense that it concerned his daily relationship to his fellowman.

Many epiphanies seem to be sparked by nature or the arts, some religious and some not. Jane Goodall in her autobiographical book, *Reasons for Hope,* writes of epiphanies that arose from her life in the natural world studying chimpanzees in Gombe. She writes that "[t]he forest—any forest—is, for me, the most spiritual place." [Goodall, 268]. About her youth, she writes of her growing spirituality as an encounter with nature:

> All the time, I was getting closer to animals and nature, and as a result, closer to myself and more and more in tune with the spiritual power that I felt all around. For those who have experienced the joy of being alone with nature there is really little need for me to say much more; for those who have not, no words of mine can ever describe the powerful, almost mystical knowledge of beauty and eternity that come, suddenly, and all unexpected. [Goodall, 72]

All the qualities of epiphany mentioned by William James are there: ineffability, noesis, transiency, and passivity.

Somewhat to my surprise, my son Brian, of no declared religion, once spoke to me about the spiritual experiences he has had while—of all things—fishing. I asked him to give me something in writing that I might feel free to excerpt, because I had never run into spiritual experiences about nature that focused not only on beauty but on fishing. He responded with a piece about the kind of epiphany he has known while fly fishing:

> This does not happen spontaneously or accidentally like a lightening strike, but is the result of many hours fishing and a complete intimacy with everything around you. It's the product of the rocks you recognize on the bottom, the flurry of bug hatches you can predict or the lay of a trout you intuitively know to be behind a certain rock. The stream must be an old friend sharing secrets....
>
> By whatever mechanism, you suddenly know the inanimate and the animate as a single entity...There is no right or wrong, there is only the benign persistence of time and existence. Perhaps it's the utter paucity of any sentient quality to the nature of existence that overcomes you—again, not intellectually, but viscerally. It is without these human superimpositions, when the intellectual templates

are lifted, that existence, or perhaps even truth, becomes tangible, even as if you were touching it or seeing it or smelling it. Beyond that, the sensation defies description, except to say that—at least for a while—you are not afraid of death.

This kind of epiphany usually stops the angler from fishing. He lingers, taking it all in, often well after dark. He gets back in the car machine and is human and segregated once more. But having touched truth, he is a more soulful creature, and thus more contented. [Brian Wiprud, from "Waving String"]

The relationship of the arts to spirituality is discussed by James immediately after his quotation about how a maxim may suddenly reveal itself to someone:

This sense of deeper significance is not confined to rational propositions. Single words, and conjunctions of words, effects of light on land and sea, odors and musical sounds, all bring it when the mind is tuned aright. Most of us can remember the strangely moving power of passages in certain poems read when we were young, irrational doorways as they were through which the mystery of fact, the wildness and the pang of life, stole into our hearts and thrilled them. The words have now perhaps become mere polished surfaces for us; but lyric poetry and music are alive and significant only in proportion as they fetch these vague vistas of a life continuous with our own, beckoning and inviting, yet ever eluding our pursuit. We are alive or dead to the eternal inner message of the arts according as we have kept or lost this mystical susceptibility. [James, 301-02]

Some music is preeminently able to bring epiphanal experiences to certain people. The passion with which some people I know—both religious and not—attend classical musical events attests to this fact. They are obviously spiritually thirsty and expect to find waters for their soul. Not every time is their thirst quenched, but they know at which spring they are most likely to find satisfaction. My son Ted, a composer of classical music, is one of these musical people. While deeply religious and a regular attendant at church services, he obviously looks to music for succor, which he intellectually connects with Christianity. He responded to my request for written testimony as follows:

> Whenever I hear the opening chorus of the *St. Matthew Passion* of J. S. Bach, the entire Passion of Christ wells up in my conscious-ness. The music focuses my mind on the central drama of Chris-tianity, and I am suddenly back in my own ongoing drama of relationship with the divine. It's uncanny: even a few measures have such a powerful effect.
>
> To some degree, it's a matter of association—music's well-known tendency to trigger memories and their attendant emotions. But what I discover in the *St. Matthew Passion*—and in countless other works, not all of them explicitly or exclusively sacred—is something deeper and richer. Like all great works, this music is a living window on the soul of its composer. When the composer is not only supremely skilled musically, but also a probing spiritual mind, the close listener receives direct and intense spiritual experi-ence, vividly replayed.
>
> Sometimes such music leads me to quiet contemplation; other times it stirs me more profoundly than prayer. It can haunt me long after the hearing, like a sermon or an encounter that gets to the heart of some unnamed longing or need. It turns over and over in my mind, teaching important truths that resist expression in words. [Theodore Wiprud]

Whatever the source of epiphany, the experience is to be found everywhere, among the religious and non-religious, the intellectual and non-intellectual—there seems to be a universal susceptibility to it. The question then arises: How do we, and how should we, react to such experiences? In response to the first part of the question, it seems that we do in fact remember them, hang onto them in our minds, and trea-sure them in our hearts. We seem to feel—and I say correctly so—that they are special to *us*, a revelation of some kind of truth that has come not to all humanity, not to the minister, not to our brilliant friend, but to *us*, insignificant though we may be in the eyes of the world.

I would suggest that we open our little jewel boxes, take out our treasured epiphanies, and think about them. They are evidence of the universe of the spirit, so easily forgotten in our busy, secular world. We get up, we go here, we go there, and then we go to sleep; and so our lives too lightly fly away, ofttimes leaving us little substance. Our epiphanies are our own special windows to the world of eternity, windows that have been entered by a "something other" that has put into several moments of our life a gift, meant just for us, crafted just for us, and available only to us. I see them as a special evidence that God, the universal Spirit, or whatever one may choose to name Him or Her, does indeed cherish us by sending exclusively to us this particular message that says, in colloquial language, "Hey—look, see, hear. You are cherished enough by me, just for who you are, so that I have come just to you to help open your eyes to the *real* world, the eternal world within your daily life. Remember this forever."

And so we will. But will we act on it or just put it into our jewel box? The moral of the story is that if we are wise, we will bring out our special jewels from their pretty little boxes and live in the truth and power they make available to us.

◆　　　◆　　　◆

The gift of an epiphany is the knowledge of being cherished by God as a unique human being with whom God wishes to be in constant contact, if we will let him. That contact, as initiated by us, is often called prayer, the subject of the next chapter.

DISCUSSION QUESTIONS

Have you ever had an epiphany, defined as an experience that defies description, seems to be authoritative, lasts a short time, and seems to come from outside you? If so, what gave rise to it?

Do you think that an individual's spiritual experience is a reliable source of truth and should influence his life?

Do you agree that the love felt when one "falls in love" or when one has a child is related to God's love for us? Consider that both experiences have to do with procreation.

6

PRAYER and BEING CHERISHED

What is more natural, and easier, if you believe in God than to address Him? How could one not? [Lewis, *Prayer*, 77]

Think of someone who cherishes you, someone you admire, to whom you are really close, and whom you trust to want only the best for you. Perhaps your mate, your mother, your sister, or your best friend. Do you need to be told how to speak with that person? No. Nor do you need to be told how, or when, or why to pray to God. I have come to realize that the source of whatever problem we may have in praying stems from our not realizing that God cherishes us. It really *is* that simple.

Let's reverse it. Think of people of whose concern and love you are not at all sure, people who are essentially indifferent or merely friendly to you. With such people, techniques and timing are useful to establish an amicable and productive relationship. We give some thought about how and when to ask our boss for a raise, how to address a group of coworkers, even how to speak to our daughter about some troubling issue. Will those well-tbought-out approaches be helpful when we speak with the special person of whose love and strength we are sure? Or might those approaches in fact insert some distance between us and that person?

I am suggesting not only that the myriad of books, sermons, manuals, and instruction of all sorts about how to pray may be unnecessary, but also that they may sometimes hinder rather than help us pray to

God. For quite a while I was attending a church whose minister was—as I phrased it to myself—"hooked" on prayer. To him, prayer was the key to all religion. So far, so good. The heart of religion *is* our personal relationship to God, which occurs primarily in prayer. My problem with his approach to the subject was that he thought that his flock needed to be taught how to pray, both silently and aloud, and instructed in what should be said. I actually found myself in a group that was practicing praying aloud in small groups, and then assessing each other's proficiency—in a kindly and encouraging way, of course. This felt to me almost sacrilegious, as if I were betraying a close relationship. Breathing a request to God for pardon, I monkeyed out what was expected.

Was my reaction shared? I think it was by some. I remember one young woman in particular who seemed taken aback, muttering something about prayer being so "personal." The general reaction, however, was insecurity among those who were not practiced in offering public prayers. Most couldn't think of what they should say, so they mimicked, as did I, the most usual public prayers. Then, ironically, they turned for more instruction and practice in "spontaneous" praying before a group.

I should say that my objection is not to public prayer, but rather to the idea of teaching anyone how to pray, whatever the situation. The most effective public prayers are those that clearly emanate from a close relationship of the speaker with God, and "should direct us to where God really is, not up but down deep." [Hart, 23] The difference between an automated prayer and one that springs from a closeness with God can be spotted one sentence into the prayer.

A related subject is the use of prayers written by others. Although we do not talk to our best friend by reading someone else's message to her, we just might send her a greeting card or a poem that expressed beautifully and exactly what we were feeling. We sometimes know a release, a sense of success where there was none before, when a prayer says precisely what we were feeling and thinking but couldn't quite get hold of.

In this way, it may even bring us more into the spirit of praying, into the sense of closeness to God that its writer felt and that comes to us as we enter into the prayer. An example of such a prayer for me is in the Episcopalian *Book of Common Prayer*: "Almighty God, unto whom all hearts are open, all desires known, and from whom no secrets are hid: Cleanse the thoughts of our hearts by the inspiration of thy Holy Spirit, that we may perfectly love thee, and worthily magnify thy holy Name; through Christ our Lord. Amen."

So if prayer is simply talking to someone who cherishes you, why all the strictures, admonitions, preachings, scribblings, and agonizing down through the ages and well into our own, all about this act called prayer? I have just finished reading or rereading a number of books, some of considerable length and most by highly respected clergymen and theologians on why, how, and when we should pray. With all due respect to their analytical and didactic skills, and also to their sincerity, I think they have overcomplicated and in fact obfuscated the central issue.

However, before listing and checking off how all the various prayer problems are solved when we become more fully aware of God's love for us personally, I should deal with the obvious differences between the *person* who cherishes us completely and the *God* who cherishes us completely, to see if the differences adversely affect our freedom to speak. And in fact the reverse is true. Unlike our best friend, God is omnipresent, always available to hear us. He also is powerful, able to do whatever he wishes and thus to help us. And he already knows what is in our hearts and minds, so we need not be embarrassed by our shortcomings and our inability to express ourselves in words. In contrast, our best friend might not be available to us at just the moment when we need to open our hearts to her, to seek her advice. We might at times tailor our way of speaking to her, so as not to hurt her feelings, but that is no consideration with God, whose self-image or ego—if one can use such terms in relation to God—will not be hurt. While we are limited in our requests to our friend by the extent of her power, obviously not so with God. And with our best friend we might hesitate to reveal some of our petty wishes and angry thoughts, for fear of shocking her or making her ashamed of us, but we know that our sins are no news to God.

Putting aside the basic hindrance to any prayer, which is our lack of trust that God really does cherish us, a common problem dealt with in detail in many books is wondering what we *should* say to him. Instructions from Jesus on how to pray, which have come down to us in the Bible as the Lord's Prayer, have been analyzed inside and out, so that ofttimes we think that we should cover each point on the list, one by one, if we could only translate the biblical language so that we will understand how the various clauses in the prayer are applicable to our daily life.

But consider. Your best friend would think you were slightly crazy if you approached her and spoke from a list. With your best friend, you speak from your heart. You say what is in your mind, you tell her what is bothering you, you confess what stupidities or horrible things you have just done and how awful you feel about them. You come to her very fast with your joys, because you instinctively know that happiness shared is doubled. Or perhaps you come to her gloating about a victory over a competitor, but you quickly sense your own selfishness as you hear yourself speak. If we can come so openly to our friend, how much more openly can we come to God. There is no "should" for prayer. C. S. Lewis puts it this way: "[W]e want to know not how we should pray if we were perfect but how we should pray being as we now are.... We must lay before Him what is in us, not what ought to be in us. [Lewis, *Prayer,* 22]

A related issue is how to find the right words to address the mighty creator of the universe. Words are often a stumblingblock, particularly to people who find them so when addressing friends about important matters. The right words just don't come to them. And when speaking to Almighty God, they feel they *should*—there's that word again—do it well. Here we come to a big difference among people. Each of us feels differently about words. Some people can chatter on about their lives and their hopes and fears to anyone, including God, while others get tongue-tied if their emotions are at all involved. Others, and this group includes me, are wordsmiths of a sort. When I try to use sentences in prayer, I find myself concentrating on grammar or the precision of a particular word. Foolish, but so it is. Ignoring words, I bring up mental images, remember, think about the future, or just turn my mind free, with an occasional word or two popping in. I really in effect turn my feelings and my thoughts toward God, wanting communion with the Mystery, to feel that I am in harmony with the spirit of creation. My praying at times could be called "thinking while aware of God's presence." Others would term this activity not prayer but "contemplation" or "meditation."

Distinctions between prayer and contemplation—and even compassionate living—become blurred. Hart describes contemplation as "this deeper vision into things, and the resultant reverence." [Hart, 22] C. S. Lewis wants to keep words *out* of his prayers: "I still think the prayer without words is the best—if one can really achieve it…. For me words are in any case secondary. They are only an anchor. Or, shall I say, they are the movements of a conductor's baton: not the music." [Lewis, *Prayer*, 11] Bishop Spong broadens prayer even further, to include all of his life: "So praying and living deeply, richly, and fully have become for me almost indistinguishable." [Spong, 144]

Another problem is when to pray. Should there be a morning prayer on awakening and an evening prayer on retiring? Again, there is no "should." Let's say that your special loved one is your mate. Would you say good morning to him and think with him about the upcoming day, particularly if you depended on him for some help that day? Nothing would be more natural. And then pillow talk in the evening would come as a matter of course, when you would tell him what had been going on and how you felt about it. Prayer is an anytime activity. As such, many religious teachers of various persuasions have felt that it is always in danger of melting from an anytime activity into a no-time activity. That certainly does happen when we lose our awareness of God's presence, which all of us do frequently. Therefore, we might as well make use of the helpful aspect of habit so that a regular time of prayer can bring back our minds to the Spirit within and around us.

A prime question among those hesitant to pray is whether or not God hears or answers prayer. We don't want to be so foolish as to address thin air or a God who isn't listening or may not respond. We worry that we are only talking to ourselves, and that if praying accomplishes anything it is the same as thinking—affecting our subconscious and nothing else. What kind of response are we looking for from God when we pray, so that we will know that he is hearing us? In our culture and our times, we are not prepared or expecting to hear an actual voice with our physical ears. In fact, we put a big question mark on the sanity of anyone who claims he does hear God making real sound waves. I think many of us, while critical of the idea that he speaks out loud to others, really hope that he will speak out loud to us. While we believe that nothing happens outside the natural order, we wish it would, just for us, so we would know that God is really listening.

Let us not be too quick to dismiss our subconscious as if it is unrelated to God, just because psychologists have determined that it is a part of the natural order, the way human beings are made. In fact, the subconscious is a prime avenue for God's communication with us. We are all aware that ideas sometimes, as we say, just "pop into our minds." So do images, memories, feelings. The subconscious is nothing new to us, verified—so to speak—by psychologists for many years. Our conscience, so well-known for centuries that it has not apparently needed specific verification, is another obvious avenue through which God reaches us. In my personal imagery, I think of God's responding as a power from beyond that comes up inside as a Spirit into the subconscious and the conscience, sometimes very quietly and often incognito. Even as we can and do pray without consciously addressing God, so do we often receive his answer without recognizing the fact.

An incident occurred to me two nights ago that exemplifies the action of the subconscious as well as our often casual treatment of its significance. I had wakened well into the night, needing a sip of water to relieve the dryness in my mouth. I hoped to turn over and fall back easily into whatever dream I had been having, but my mind insisted on thinking about the writing of this book. One idea came that I liked, and I thought, "That's fine. I hope I'll remember it, and now I want to go back to sleep." Unbidden, more ideas, more words kept coming up into my sleepy mind. I recognized that, unlike some middle-of-the-night thoughts, these were to the point. But I wanted to go back to sleep, so I would be rested enough to write well in the morning. I definitely did *not* want to get waylaid into thinking about my writing in the middle of the night. Then it came to me that I was, in effect, telling God to be quiet so I could go to sleep. Although in the morning I was going to begin this chapter on prayer, I hadn't the common sense to realize that help was coming up from God through my subconscious. At that point, I grinned to myself, loosened up, welcomed the ideas and words as they bubbled up, and before long went back to sleep. Of course, writing about spirituality and religion, I had often prayed for inspiration from God, and this was part of his answer, although given at a time that I unthankfully found inconvenient.

What if I had not recognized that this was God responding to my prayers? Would that have made it less of a response? No, not really. Which leads me to another point—that we sometimes communicate with God, both ways, without terming it prayer. Even if we do not say, "God, please help me now," we instinctively reach out toward something way out there and also way inside us. In fact, we need not even intellectually think there *is* a God. Remember the statement that there are no atheists in foxholes? Martin Buber expresses the same idea in terms of his particular theology: "But when he, too, who abhors the name, and believes himself to be godless, gives his whole being to addressing the *Thou* of his life, as a *Thou* that cannot be limited by another, he addresses God." [Buber, 76] We need not have experienced fear in a foxhole to be aware that for most human beings prayer becomes automatic when they are in danger. We turn to God and say, "Please, please, God, don't let this happen!" Or something similar. This widespread tendency to turn without thought to some superior Being strongly suggests that people at such times are accepting the Spirit without realizing what they are doing.

Prayer does not have to be a matter of kneeling down, trying to concentrate on God, and framing a request. The less it is like that, the better. The more we force our minds to concentrate on our prayer and some image of God, the less receptive we are apt to be to what may come into our minds, just by chance. And that chance, of course, is one of God's avenues to us. As in our communication with our best friend, we must at times stop talking and simply listen.

Perhaps the double question most discussed about prayer is whether we should petition God to give us something or intercede with him to help someone else; and then, whether he can and will disrupt the natural order of things to respond to our petitionary and intercessory prayers. My answer to the first part is: How can we not speak to God about something of great concern to us, even as we would to our best friend? There is no "should." If we trust in God's love for us personally, we will of course unburden our hearts of our desires and concerns. Hart expands this idea by saying that often "prayer is the only expression available to us of the love we have for someone. It is our bond of unity with them." [Hart, 105]

My answer to the second question is equally simple: We don't know, nor do we need to know how he will "answer" our prayers. We know God is powerful, we know he loves us and others, and so we must ask. The rest is up to him. I would only comment that, even assuming that God acts only through the natural order, our prayer forms a part of the natural order in that it *is* a happening. In short, we pray for help for ourselves and others because it is in our heart to do so. Once again Spong phrases the situation well, pointing out its possibilities:

> Perhaps we human beings are more psychologically connected than we have ever imagined. Perhaps positive thoughts and the release of the energy of concern does flow on networks we do not understand, affecting the life of another. These transformations seem to be miraculous only inside our limited knowledge. All I know is that it is natural to reach out, to love, and to care for others, and inevitably we feel compelled to give verbal expression to those aspects of our lives. [Spong, 145]

We do not need to know if petitionary and intercessory prayer "work" in the sense that we would have them do so, but it is important that we recognize that we cannot prove that they don't, and therefore we cannot dismiss the possibility.

My theme in this chapter has been that prayer is spontaneous and frequent, in the same way conversation is with a best friend, when we know that God cherishes us. You may have noticed that I have been using the word "cherish" instead of "love" when it fit into the context. Although almost synonymous with the many-faceted and quite general word "love," it has specific connotations of protecting someone as a precious and unique individual.

And of course *there* is the problem. How do we learn to know that God cherishes us? And until we know that, might not the various prayer techniques and instructions be useful? I hesitate to admit it, but yes, they might, for some people and at some period in their lives, while for others they act as a hindrance. We are all different.

So, if knowing that God cherishes us is the key to prayer, how do we come to an experiential knowledge of this? Very briefly at this point, I want to suggest several ways. First, but probably not most important, many of the world's religions carry this message in one form or another. Specifically in our culture, the Christian tradition tells us that God came into the world in Jesus to make it completely clear that God cherishes us. To put it mildly, reading or hearing this message is not a surefire road to accepting the truth of it into our lives. Intellectual affirmation is not enough.

A second more powerful way is personal experience. We are helped tremendously to be able to accept this message if someone in our own lives has really cherished us, for ourselves, for who we are and even for who we aren't. With luck, one or both parents will have cherished us, and we will be on the road. For most of us, however, our parents may have been well-meaning and indeed loved us in their fashion, but somehow never quite freed themselves enough from their own insecurities and ego needs to have been able to focus on us and direct that special type of love toward us that is "cherishing." I suspect that most of us fall into this group.

Meanwhile, that cherishing sort of love is rampant in the world. I use the word "rampant" to indicate that there is lots of it out there, that it is a powerful, energetic force, and that it is unpredictable. I refer, of course, to the Spirit, God's Spirit as it flows through certain people to us and others, and that we may become aware of as the Eternal Now, discussed more fully in chapter four. We may see its manifestations in someone else and begin to understand, or we may be lucky and find that best friend I have been talking about.

And there is still another way, which I dealt with in chapter five. We may fall in love and be lucky enough to experience not merely erotic love but also an overwhelming cherishing love toward our beloved. Failing that, we may be introduced to this experience when we receive a child of our own. God sends his Spirit of love into our hearts in extreme form at such times, most notably and interestingly in those that involve our own procreation. Such experiences of his Spirit, termed epiphanies, remain in our minds and hearts. They are God's special messages to us and us alone, sent in the form most adapted to the unique creature that we are.

We are God's children. Even as we cherish our children, so does God cherish us. So how can we not, in Paul's words, "pray constantly"? [1 Thess: 5:17]

♦   ♦   ♦

For Christians or people living in a predominantly Christian culture, the concept of God's love for each of us is based on Jesus and his life, the subject of the next chapter.

DISCUSSION QUESTIONS

Have you, or have you had, a "best friend" to whom you could tell anything?

Do you find public prayers helpful? If so, do you prefer those read in unison or by a minister?

Do you use a prayer book at home? Does it help you to pray, or does it only remind you of God and what you might do to obey him?

Do you pray for others, and if so, is this instinctive or do you make a point of remembering to do so?

Did you feel that your parents "cherished" you as a unique human being? If you are a parent, do you so cherish your own children?

7

JESUS and MIRACLES

It would require much exotic calculation…to deny that the single most powerful figure—not merely in these two millenniums but in all human history—has been Jesus of Nazareth…. [A] serious argument can be made that no one else's life has proved remotely as powerful and enduring as that of Jesus. It's an astonishing conclusion in light of the fact that Jesus was a man who lived a short life in a rural backwater of the Roman Empire, who died in agony as a convicted criminal, and who may never have intended so much as a small portion of the effects worked in his name. [Reynolds Price, 86]

"But who do you say that I am?" I could not resist beginning this chapter with Jesus's own question to the disciples after hearing their reports from others concerning his identity. In response, Peter declares that Jesus is "the Christ, the Son of the living God." And Jesus praises him, saying that this knowledge has been given him by "my Father who is in heaven." So, does that settle it?

Obviously not, particularly in these skeptical and scholarly times. We have to know, first of all, what was meant at the time of writing by the term "Christ," then by the noun "Son," and finally by "my Father who is in heaven." Even if those words were verified as an accurate translation of words actually spoken by Jesus—and the scholars are doubtful—we would remain with the question as to whether or not Jesus himself knew the answer and (if we are dyed-in-the-wool skeptics) whether, if he did, he was being honest. In other words, we have to know the answer before we ask the question in order to take the answer as truth. Jesus lived two thousand years ago and the stories about his life in the Gospels were written over one hundred years after he died. So we are back where we started.

The question often arises very specifically as to whether or not Jesus was unique, whether he was the one and only Son of God, the perfect revelation of God, completely one with God. I like the way Borg comments on his own belief that Jesus, "rather than being the exclusive revelation of God,…is one of many mediators of the sacred. Yet even as this view subtracts from the uniqueness of Jesus and the Christian tradition, it also in my judgment adds to the credibility of both." [Borg, *Jesus*, 37]

As I am saying so often in these chapters, in one way or another: To our daily spiritual life, do the answers to these questions about Jesus matter? I can hear accusations of heresy, but consider the idea seriously for a moment that we do not have to comprehend exactly the relationship of Jesus to God or to the long-heralded savior of the Jewish people at that time. The Gospels continually show Jesus pointing to what he does, to his acts, not discoursing on who he is. He talks about God as his father and as the father of us all, but even there he resists theology. He speaks of what God has done, is doing, and will do. He uses parables about people for this purpose rather than statements of fact. He knew instinctively what Thomas Hart noted that G. K. Chesterton remarked centuries later, namely, that "there are only two things that satisfy the soul: a person and a story. Then he adds that even a story has to be about a person." [Hart, 51] Borg notes that "stories appeal to the imagination, to that place within us where our images of reality, of life, and ourselves reside." [Borg, *Jesus*, 121] So Jesus does not say that God is loving, but instead tells the parable of the prodigal son and himself acts toward everyone he meets with total empathy and compassion. With Jesus, it seemed to have been life in action, not statements about that life. Such statements would be made in abundance after his death.

So perhaps we should look at Jesus first in the way that it seems he wanted us to, namely, at what he did and how he approached living.

We read in the Gospels that he was extraordinarily compassionate, healing with what seemed to his disciples like miracles despite the dangers of so doing; he associated with anyone, regardless of social status, ignoring the criticism he received for it; he prayed privately, never leading his disciples in prayer, although once giving them a sample prayer; and he preached continually about what God is like and what he expects of us. In Hart's words, "Jesus teaches and models the way of life that brings us into the deepest harmony with the Mystery." [Hart, 83] If you reread the Gospels, you may be struck as I have been by some of the nonsentimental, hard-nosed sayings of Jesus. He was a down-and-out realist, basing his advice on the way God's world is, not on the way we as human beings believe it should be. Usually, he finishes a precept by explaining how it will benefit the listener. For example, listen to these few excerpts from the Sermon on the Mount:

> Make friends quickly with your accuser, while you are going with him to court, lest your accuser hand you over to the judge, and the judge to the guard, and you be put in prison; truly, I say to you, you will never get out till you have paid the last penny. [Matt. 5:25-26]
>
> For he [God] makes the sun rise on the evil and on the good, and sends rain on the just and on the unjust. For if you love those who love you, what reward have you? [Matt. 5:45-46]
>
> And which of you by being anxious can add one cubit to his span of life? [Matt. 6:27]
>
> Judge not, that you be not judged. For with the judgement you pronounce you will be judged, and the measure you give will be the measure you get. [Matt. 7:1-2]

The picture of Jesus that we receive in the Gospels is of an exceptionally charismatic, authoritative, compassionate, intuitive, realistic, and spiritually powerful man. The "spiritually powerful" aspect not only brought a group of disciples to him during his life, but—and this is the remarkable part—also after he was dead; and then it somehow eventually led to establishment of a religion that has survived two thousand years. And could it be that Jesus actually *did* nothing remarkable for his time except be who he was? Other people are famous for what they produced of note or how they affected their societies during their lifetimes. Jesus never led an army, he never wrote a book or even a poem, he never painted a picture or created a sculpture, he constructed no memorable building, he never composed music. He had no special expertise and produced no "work" that would last beyond his lifetime. No one even put anything in writing about him until about forty years after his death. It was the power of his personality, his spirit, that made him so memorable and influential from his time to ours. How spiritually powerful can you get?

Of course, what occurred that gave the initial impetus to the Christian movement was, first of all, the resurrection. And here we have another difficult concept, intimately connected to the subject of miracles. Did Jesus really rise from the dead? Again, I shall give the perhaps by now irritating response: Does it matter to us as we live our lives today? Do we have to make up our minds on the answer in order to live a rewarding spiritual life? Obviously, I think not, but I do think we need to recognize the existence of an exceptional power in the man Jesus. Even the most skeptical scholars have recently been pointing out that *something* very special must have happened to spark the beginning of the Christian movement, given the danger of being a follower of Jesus after his crucifixion for largely political reasons.

The second pivotal event after Jesus's death (his resurrection being the first) was the "coming of the Holy Spirit" on what is now commemorated as the day of Pentecost. The apostles "were all filled with the Holy Spirit and began to speak in other tongues, as the Spirit gave them utterance." This was the event, recorded in the second chapter of Acts, that gave the apostles a new, almost explosive, power to preach, heal, and perform miracles. They identified this Spirit with Jesus.

Everyone who reads the Gospels with care and for counsel has his or her own take on Jesus, and I am no exception. What I find in the story of his life that is most meaningful to me in my own, is that absolute love and absolute power are combined in God. Or, stated perhaps too succinctly but very practically, love works. The world is so made that the only way that human beings can be spiritually fulfilled (happy) is by being compassionate and understanding toward each other; and, furthermore, that when we express this love it has a tremendous power to transform, to change other people, so that they in turn become more loving. Here is a train I want to take. It is going in the right direction.

For me, Jesus himself is the primary evidence and example of the fact that love and power are combined in God, which means that love is an extremely powerful force in our life. Living centuries after Jesus and his gospel of love, we may tend to forget that it is far from obvious that the creator of the world is a loving god and that therefore love reigns supreme in the world. Think about it. Would you credit a loving god with the destruction of human beings through hurricanes? How about the evil in men's natures that erupts in the torture and killing of each other and of other animals? Or look at the killing among the other creatures: would a loving God create the world so that wolves kill and eat lambs, while crocodiles snatch small animals as they approach the streams to drink? This is not a world where the love of its creator can be assumed.

But Jesus said time and again that God the creator is not only a just but a loving God. He did not explain how that could be. He simply asserted it. Jesus himself lived a life of love and was killed as a result. That does not sound like power, unless it is literally true that the creator of the physical world did raise the body as well as the spirit of Jesus from the dead. I tend to think this happened, but it is not crucial to my daily life. The important aspect is that the *spirit* of Jesus *did* return to life, filled and activated his disciples, and has permeated our world ever since as a powerful force. And is available to you and me. Jesus's preachings, life, and spiritual resurrection (at the least) tell me that if I want to be happy, to be spiritually fulfilled, I must feel and act with compassion toward other creatures. Preliminary evidence to the contrary ofttimes, this approach to each day's living will work amazingly well, simply because that is the way the world has been created.

So far, I have been stepping cautiously around the question of whether miracles—including the resurrection—really happened for Jesus and his disciples and continue to happen today. Much attention has been given to this subject over the years. One must of course begin with a definition of what we mean by a miracle. A dictionary definition that fulfills the ordinary understanding of the word is: "An event or effect in the physical world deviating from the laws of nature." C. S. Lewis, in his amusing and perceptive little book, *Miracles: A Preliminary Study*, defines it as "an interference with Nature by supernatural power." [Lewis, *Miracles*, 7]

"Nature" in the above definitions can be translated as the universe as created. The "laws" are what we human beings in our scientific inquiries have surmised and sometimes proved to represent the way the universe works. Years and years ago, Saint Augustine put it succinctly: "Miracles do not happen in contradiction to nature, but only in contradiction to that which is known to us of nature." Already some doubt has been inserted about whether or not we—even today—would be able to assert clearly what the laws of nature really are. How do we know for certain that one of those supposed laws has been broken? We don't, really, but in a practical situation we feel we do know. If a chair suddenly rises from the floor without being lifted by anybody or anything, we know that this is a miracle, in that our laws of nature do not allow for such occurrences. And yet such things are certainly reported, and often not as miracles of God, but as examples of levitation, a widely accepted phenomenon not without an aura of charlatanism. And in Jesus's day, people knew even less about how events should occur if they were not interfered with by the supernatural.

Furthermore, at that time miracles were expected from any prophet or man of God. Jesus was far from the only so-called miraculous healer of the day. Add to this the fact that the writers of the Gospels were try-ing to make it clear that Jesus was the expected savior sent from God, and it would be surprising if miracles by Jesus were *not* reported. Most of the miracles reported were healings, where the psychological aspect of health might have been involved. Increasingly today, the importance of the spiritual/psychological situation is being recognized as a major factor of healing, so perhaps what Jesus's contemporaries called mira-cles, we today, if we had been there, would have interpreted as a phe-nomenon of Jesus's spiritual power.

Personally, I do not find it difficult to accept the idea that the spiri-tual power of Jesus, received from God the creator, could affect an aspect of that creation, particularly if love and power are seen as com-bined in God. However, while not finding the idea of miracles difficult to accept, I couldn't care less whether or not Jesus's actions were mira-cles in the definition given. Back to how it affects my daily living. Not at all. I admit that I would be mightily surprised if the funneling of God's spirit of love through me or anyone I know resulted in an identi-fiable miracle of any sort, and I certainly wouldn't count on it. But you never know. Remember Hamlet's comment to Horatio about there being more things in this world than he had ever dreamed of?

I can't leave the subject of miracles without commenting on the pre-sumption of us human beings to even consider fully defining the laws of nature and on our silliness at pointing to a healing or an act of levi-tation as a breaking of that law, or a miracle. The fact is—and I would like to shout it sometimes—the *entire universe* is a miracle, in the sense that it is too marvelous for us, we cannot really understand it. Our sci-entists describe little parts of it, each one only comprehending his or her little part. I am referring to just the physical aspects of the universe, from the tiny, submicroscopic bits to its perhaps unending extension in space, and the way it all interrelates. The best of our scientists have been in awe. Thich Nhat Hanh, a Buddhist monk, mystic, and author of the currently popular *Living Buddha, Living Christ*, puts it this way:

> People usually consider walking on water
> or in thin air a miracle.
> But I think the real miracle
> is not to walk either on water or in thin air,
> but to walk on earth.
> [Sanders, introductory quotation]

Then consider the spiritual aspects of the universe, and their interaction with the physical. How can a blade of grass in a neighboring field affect your spirit? You glance around at all the other green things growing nearby and interacting with it, and perhaps you see an insect or two living nearby. You think about the sun and rain nourishing your blade of grass. Perhaps you begin to wonder how many blades of grass are right now growing in the world. And how many have grown since the beginning of it all. Soon you are ready to write a psalm, or perhaps to hear in your mind the beautiful phrases of Psalm 24, beginning with: "The earth is the Lord's and the fulness thereof, the world and those who dwell therein." [Ps. 24:1] Or the last two verses of Psalm 65: "The pastures of the wilderness drip, the hills gird themselves with joy, the meadows clothe themselves with flocks, the valleys deck themselves with grain, they shout and sing together for joy." [Ps. 65:12-13]

So much for miracles. We live in the midst of miracles and in fact are miracles ourselves. Whether or not we think that Jesus turned wine into water at a particular feast makes no difference. Because of his life and teachings, we can know our acts of love and compassion will have the power to create the real "miracle" in our world, an unquenchable movement of love outward to our mate, our children, our community, our country, and every person and creature in the whole wide world.

◆   ◆   ◆

Jesus's emphasis on compassion as God's will for mankind raises the question of whether in fact religion is necessary at all, as long as we act with goodwill toward everyone. In other words, is a system of ethics all we need? This issue is discussed in the next chapter.

DISCUSSION QUESTIONS

How would it matter to your daily life if you discarded or ignored the concept that Jesus was the one and only son of God?

Do you think that spiritual power, such as Jesus had, can affect the physical world? Is the physical resurrrection of Jesus important to you?

What in life seems to you to be the most amazing miracle of all?

8

ETHICS and COMPASSION

When we survey the whole field of religion, we find a great variety in the thoughts that have prevailed there; but the feelings on the one hand and the conduct on the other are almost always the same, for Stoic, Christian, and Buddhist saints are practically indistinguishable in their lives. [James, 390]

If one is kind to others, honest, and hard-working, isn't that enough? Is it necessary to be concerned with one's soul, to be "religious," and even to belong to a community of worship? In other words, are ethics enough? Can we be fulfilled by just living by what our society generally agrees is a moral way of life, with no effort to become spiritually aware? Will this bring us happiness? Many people, even some belonging to religious groups, would answer "yes."

Interestingly, His Holiness the Dalai Lama (his title on book jackets), would agree, at least in part. As the "spiritual and temporal leader of the Tibetan people," the Dalai Lama states bluntly, "I have come to the conclusion that whether or not a person is a religious believer does not matter much. Far more important is that they [sic] be a good human being." [DL, 19] He does emphasize spirituality, which he writes is "concerned with those qualities of the human spirit—such as love and compassion, patience, tolerance, forgiveness, contentment, a sense of responsibility, a sense of harmony—which bring happiness to both self and others." [DL, 22] He believes that the individual's search for happiness is what should provide the impetus toward ethical behavior: "[E]stablishing binding ethical principles is possible when we take as our starting point the observation that we all desire happiness and wish to avoid suffering." [DL, 28] The thesis of *Ethics for the New Millenium* is that religious belief is not necessary for ethical conduct. The Dalai Lama's emphasis is on compassion as the primary virtue, which will by its very nature lead to ethical conduct. Do you hear echoes of the New Testament, where love (properly translated as compassion) is lauded as the source of moral behavior?

If you have read this far, you know that I agree with the Dalai Lama that what we believe with our minds about God and the universe doesn't really matter very much and neither does our religious affiliation or lack of it. It is our experience of the Spirit, the Ground of our Being, that leads to compassion and then on to happiness. In his effort to avoid all religious flavor, the Dalai Lama skips over spiritual experience, at least in those terms. He does, however, recognize the usefulness of religions, clearly stating that "the spiritual qualities of love and compassion…are most easily and effectively developed within the context of religious practice." [DL, 220] It is worth noting that, according to a Gallup survey in 1996, U.S. religious institutions are the major source of community volunteers and their members are far likelier than others to donate to charities. [Gallup, 1996, quoted in W. Gallagher, 10] Following the thought that compassion is the goal, William James points out, in the lead quote for this chapter, that the religious feelings and actions of saints of all religions and philosophies are virtually the same.

So what about the "good man" who not only eschews all religion but also never considers his spiritual condition, and yet who nevertheless lives a relatively blame-free life according to his standards and those of his community? I return to the theme: We are all different. For some of us, that would not be enough. We want, indeed need, to have a sense of harmony with the Spirit, to feel the breeze blowing at least occasionally. We are made that way. The "good man" is made another way. We are all in a sense different animals, who with any luck reach the same goal of compassion for other creatures and the happiness and fulfillment that follows. The difference is primarily that the "good man" is not as conscious of the elements of his experience and does not try to define them. And the exact nature of his experience may differ because of who he is, including his genetic makeup, early life, and education. He does not speak the name of God, but may nevertheless partake of God's spirit of love. Each of us is a unique creation. What we share is a nature that only finds happiness, only knows fulfillment, through the spiritual experience of compassion.

If the spirit of compassion powers ethics, more needs to be said about it here. You will note that I am using the word "compassion" instead of "love," because that aspect of "love"—a very general term with many different meanings—that we are considering is really compassion, which means literally a "feeling with." Marcus Borg describes it as "feeling the feelings of somebody else in a visceral way, at a level somewhere below the level of the head." [Borg, *Jesus*, 47] He underlines its importance: "As the primary gift of the Spirit, compassion is the primary sign of spiritual growth." [Borg, *God*, 129]

There is much agreement as to how compassion expresses itself, put most familiarly in Paul's "hymn to love": "Love is patient and kind; love is not jealous or boastful; it is not arrogant or rude. Love does not insist on its own way; it is not irritable or resentful; it does not rejoice at wrong, but rejoices in the right. Love bears all things, believes all things, hopes all things, endures all things. Love never ends..." [1 Cor. 13:4-8]

Undoubtedly, anyone who has such love is a happy, contented, fulfilled person. Few of us would deny that. The problem, of course, is how to attain that state of heart and mind. How do we become truly compassionate? What are the ingredients of compassion for us in our everyday lives? How do we learn to think of others before ourselves, and then how do we discern what will lead to others' happiness?

A theological—and, to my way of thinking, accurate—answer is that we must access the Spirit that is the Ground of our Being and act in harmony with it, allow ourselves to go with the flow of love that we experience. Yes, indeed. But what does that really mean? What does it mean when I find myself angry, impatient, jealous, aggressive, ambitious, greedy, arrogant, lonely, or fearful? What we need is a non-theological, practical answer as to how we start, day after day, to make ourselves become more compassionate.

I have found four rather distinct but interconnected ways of moving toward compassion. Unfortunately, the first is the most elusive as well as the most important in terms of making the remaining three more possible, although they can be effective on their own. The first is faith. It is hard to consider other people at all if we are very worried about ourselves. An extreme example is a drowning person, who of course cannot think about anyone else. He is intent on saving himself. This is natural, an example of the self-preservation instinct that we all know in our daily lives in less urgent but persistent fashion. If, however, we have come to trust God in the sense that we know that he cherishes us, is all-powerful, and knows what is happening to even the tiniest sparrow, then we can feel secure enough to turn outward. This has nothing to do with belief in God's existence, and everything to do with trust in God's love and power on a personal scale. I may think in terms of Ground of Being, Mystery, etc., but I nevertheless personally find it helpful to visualize the large hand of God upholding a small person, me. I think there is a famous drawing very like that. If indeed I am being watched over, upheld, then I am free to turn outward toward others.

A common example of how trust leads to consideration of others occurs in the raising of our children. A child who really knows herself loved and secure can begin to turn outward as her infant self-preservation instincts gradually become less acute. She can hand the first cookie to her friend if she knows that her mother has another cookie and will give her one. She trusts in both her mother's power and her love. Note that neither love alone nor power alone will do it. A child may know herself loved by her parents but feel insecure for any number of reasons, such as a changing household, no dependable routine, inconsistent rules, and insufficient discipline. Such a child has unconscious fears that her parents are not all-powerful, and she will be slower to turn outward toward others and to develop such characteristics as generosity, friendliness, and adaptability. She may notice that showing those virtues produces praise and other rewards, and so begin to mimic them, but she will not be able honestly to experience them in her heart. And so with us adults. We need to trust that an all-powerful God knows what is going on with us and will take care of us according to his wisdom, if not our desires.

Once our self-preservation instincts have been relaxed, we can turn outward towards others more easily. The second way of moving toward compassion can then come into play. It involves both imagination and feelings. We can develop empathy, which literally means "feeling into." Empathy occurs when we imagine ourselves in the skin of the other guy, note how we would be feeling if we were he, and feel an echo of that feeling within ourselves.

The Dalai Lama writes that we have an "innate capacity for empathy," [DL, 77] which can be developed by "sustained reflection," followed by "rehearsal and practice." [DL, 74] It may be that our capacity for empathy is shared to some extent by several of what we term the "higher animals," but there is no doubt that it is a particularly human ability. The first ingredient is imagination, the facility of pretending in our minds that we *are* someone else. Young children exhibit this ability to varying degrees, the most obvious example being a little girl's delight in playing with dolls, imagining for the moment that she is a mother. A small boy might more likely pretend to be the driver of a toy truck. Such imagining diminishes with years, of course, or at least becomes less obvious. The point is that we all have the ability.

The trick is to use it in relation to another person. Our mother may tell us as we are growing up and perhaps exhibiting selfishness or anger toward another person, to "think about how *he* (or she) feels." Exhortation is rarely an effective tool, however, and a much better one exists for that mother who wants her little one to develop empathy. The tool is stories, primarily fiction. A child who develops a taste for stories learns to imagine himself inside another person, albeit a fictional one. Stories are universally appealing. The G. K. Chesterton remark, quoted earlier, is again a propos, to the effect that only two things satisfy the soul—a person and a story, and that even the story has to be about people.

I emphasize fiction because books that describe how someone feels about his experiences, as if the author were inside that person, are usually fictional, although they may be autobiographical or, as in a biography, based on fact. If you live into a novel that does a fine job of portraying the feelings of someone very different from you in situations that you yourself have never experienced, you will be stretching your empathetic muscles, so to speak. Not only will you be able to feel into someone you meet in real life who resembles the person in the novel in both type and situation, but you will be developing the ability to feel into people in general. Fiction, with the opportunities it affords to develop empathy, is of course present not only in books, but also in realistic plays on stage and television.

Being able to empathize with another person and doing it are two different matters. The Dalai Lama is correct that practice is required for empathy to become a way of thought. We tend to be much more aware of how *we* are feeling than how the other guy may be feeling. We have to take ourselves by the collar, so to speak, and make ourselves think and feel into the thoughts and feelings of that other guy. The more we do it, the more capable we become and the more we will tend to do it automatically. In fact, the habit of empathy can at times be felt by our self-seeking selves as a nuisance. Just when we were enthusiastically considering how angry we were because Henry had made a slighting remark about our cooking, we find that something inside us has said, "Come on, you know perfectly well why he said that. He is feeling small and needs to feel like a big guy who knows something about good food." With luck, we will say to ourselves, "Sure, that's right. He isn't thinking about you and your cooking at all, really. This is his problem and you should try to buck up his ego a little by saying something he is wanting to hear." But there is a tiny part that may just miss the emotional excitement of being angry, which can sometimes be rather exhilarating for a little while. Our egos have some momentary fun when we are paying them our full attention.

While remarking upon the dark side of our natures, I should also note that empathy does not *always* lead to compassionate feelings or actions. The ability to understand another's feelings can be used for one's own advantage. While it may result in good characteristics, like patience, tact, and the other virtues noted in 1 Corinthians, it may also be used to manipulate another person. Empathy is a powerful tool.

So, assuming that we are going to use our empathic skills to become compassionate, should we kowtow to whatever we perceive that the other guy would like us to do? No, and this is where things become more complicated. Compassion involves judgment, which is a third, and sometimes neglected component. Let's take Henry, so critical of my cooking. Should we really try to buck up his ego about his gourmet abilities? That would certainly be the easiest and most obvious way to go, but it is a possibility that if we do so we will just be encouraging him to make disparaging remarks about other people's cooking, and so make him unpopular with them. And onward down the cycle of insecurity for poor Henry.

I am reminded of what I think was a correct judgment call made by my son Ted in his teen years. It surprised me at the time. A classmate, who in my generation would have been called a "sad sack," but in this generation would be called a "nerd," had decided that he wanted Ted as his very special friend. Both boys shared academic ability and several classes, but little else. The classmate, whom I shall call Gerald, had been trying to arrange increasingly frequent get-togethers with my son, who had obliged him in several instances. Ted and I agreed that we felt sorry for Gerald for a number of reasons, and that his doing things occasionally with him was part of being kind to others. Then one day, my son turned round on the issue. Gerald had telephoned him asking him to come along with him and his mother while he bought some shoes. Ted said no, apparently with some finality, and Gerald rarely called him after that. The relationship had reached a point where it was no longer good for Gerald, much less Ted, to continue it. Gerald had started to lean on Ted and take advantage of his kindness, which I know Gerald was smart enough to perceive as such. Ted, though young, was able to perceive the imbalance that had developed, and pulled out, even though his action could have been called unkind. In this example, Ted did empathize with Gerald, continuing to understand his need for friendship, but judgment entered the scene and he realized that doing just what Gerald wanted was not in the end helpful to Gerald. In fact, it was just the opposite, preventing him from learning to develop mutually rewarding relationships.

The moral of the story is that we cannot and should not turn off our minds. Back to the Dalai Lama, who wrote that "the moral value of a given act is to be judged in relation both to time, place, and circumstance and to the interests of the totality of all others in the future as well as now." [DL, 153] Many times it is far easier just to do what we perceive in our empathy that someone else feels he needs us to do, than to consider whether, under the circumstances, it may not be helpful to that person. And we know that our judgment may be wrong. Nevertheless it is our responsibility to try to make a judgment. The person who is always obliging tends to be considered by the world as kind, whereas a refusal to oblige someone's wishes may be perceived as unkind. We do like our praise from others.

The use of our minds in conjunction with our compassion is also necessary in our social and political actions, as distinct from our relationship with individual persons. I have found that many "good people" and in fact many churches automatically assume that compassion in a political sense means helping the poor and the suffering, without considering which method will do the job best. Should this compassion be expressed in the form of action by some arm of the government, by industry, by private charities, or by the individual? Should it take the form of a donation, a loan, or some scheme involving education and self-help? Many questions must be answered concerning the best way to exercise compassion socially and politically. Often people will choose the easiest answer, putting the onus on the federal government, which may or may not be the best, depending very much upon each individual problem. Marcus Borg points out that "a politics of compassion is not a particular set of specific economic and social policies but a social vision that is to affect all of our political thinking. How best to implement and incarnate that vision is to a large extent a pragmatic question of what works best to reach that goal." [Borg, *God,* 150]

It is unfortunate that a number of religious congregations have become so enthusiastic in their desire to exercise compassion toward those in physical need that they completely neglect the spiritual needs of their own members. They have a tendency to jump on the bandwagon of some well-organized charitable effort or even of a political party, forgetting that their primary goal is to provide spiritual succor and guidance. There is room for both efforts, and more perceptive leaders and groups do realize that the source of the most effective and lasting social action is the compassion of the individual spirit.

There remains still one other way to move toward compassion, rather shallow but nonetheless useful. In addition to trying to rely on God's concern for us (faith), to learn to feel into others (empathy), and to use our intelligence about what really seems to be helpful to others (judgment), we can try imitation as a technique. Our minds, spirits, and bodies are fantastically complex and interconnected. Sometimes things work that according to our scientific knowledge, such as it is, make no sense. Nevertheless, they do work, and if we are aware that they might, we should give them a try.

I remember vividly the surprise I experienced as a beginner on the ski slopes when I first discovered that imitation works. Now, I am not well-coordinated physically at all, and thus my first instinct when learning a sport is to analyze exactly how it is done and give specific instructions to my body parts. I rely on my mind, having learned that my body isn't naturally as cooperative as most other people's. So after awkwardly trying to do the stem christie several times, noting that my body should face this way, my skis—left and right—should be here, and my poles still somewhere else, I sort of gave up and decided—what the heck!—I would just *do* it. Couldn't be worse. I turned off my ever-analyzing mind and just threw myself into an imitation of my instructor's body. And I did it, I actually got through the stem christie without falling. I had performed the maneuver she had demonstrated simply by pretending my body was hers and letting it do its thing. Imitation. How easy, how non-intellectual, how exciting.

I need to add that my attempts at the stem christie did not always prove successful afterwards, by a long shot, but my body had the know-how tucked away somewhere, and I realized that with practice I really could do it. It would be nice to add that I went on to become a proficient downhill skier, but that did not happen, because my opportunities to ski were very limited in those days in Washington, D.C., with four little children at home.

Our spirits, like our bodies, can be great imitators. We can imitate others who are compassionate. The prime example of a compassionate person for our culture is of course Jesus. When we read of his actions and words in the New Testament, we are challenged to try to feel into what he was feeling and thinking—empathy—but also, and with equal importance, simply to imitate him. He ate with people who in his day were considered "sinners," an action that we can imitate. He healed people's bodies, minds, and spirits, showing a concern that we can imitate, although with less effectiveness. Most important, he focused his entire life on following God's will for him, an approach to living that can also be imitated.

Knowing as much as we can about Jesus's life, his actions and words, is therefore important. Biblical scholars for more than a century have been researching the customs during Jesus's lifetime and the circumstances leading to the writing of the Gospels, in an effort to draw an increasingly accurate picture of the man Jesus. A current group working on discerning which sayings of Jesus are most authentic, most likely to have been passed down to us with accuracy, is called The Jesus Seminar.

Imitation is not the real thing, of course, but it has a way of giving birth to the real thing. This transformation is to me one of the greatest miracles of life. From nothing comes something. I may in no way feel friendly toward another woman, but if I act as if I like her—i.e., imitate the approach of a friendly person—and do this often enough, I find that somehow or other my attitude toward her has changed. I actually have begun to like her, almost in spite of myself. An example of what is termed "grace," a gift, an unearned benefit.

Our "good man" toward the beginning of this chapter may or may not be imitating compassionate people and thus moving toward becoming one himself. He may simply be following precepts, rules, and standards of conduct laid out by his parents and community. While what he believes about the existence of God and the divinity of Jesus hardly affect his development of compassion, will following rules, by itself, do so? The evidence is against it. Such rules are examples of the legalism that was repeatedly seen as insufficient throughout the New Testament. Standards of conduct are certainly useful before compassion develops, and they serve as a guide when we cannot find compassion in our hearts. And perhaps at times, like imitation, they may give rise to the real thing. However, they are too rigid to adapt to the reality we run into every day, and thus are no substitute for the spirit of compassion that understands another person and situation.

Happiness is a spiritual state. Ethical standards have nothing to do with the human spirit. Compassion, however, is an attitude of the spirit that leads not only to what we call ethical behavior, but also to the spiritual fulfillment that we term happiness. Working day by day to become more compassionate is the way to happiness. Whatever helps us toward this end is worth trying.

◆   ◆   ◆

So far, we have been looking primarily at the rosy side of life: trust in a loving and powerful God, experiences of the Spirit, the Eternal Now of life, and compassion as seen in Jesus. We have only alluded slightly to the dark side, so the next chapter will look at the thorny problems of how a God of compassion can have created a world so prone to natural disaster and human beings who so often kill each other mercilessly.

DISCUSSION QUESTIONS

If you are indeed kind, honest, and hard-working, do you need also to be religious in order to be happy? What, if anything, would (or does) religion add? Is religion necessary as a support for ethical conduct?

Can you name more ways of increasing compassion, in addition to faith, empathy, judgment, and imitation? How necessary to the other three is the first, faith?

Give examples of how one can learn to feel empathy more often toward others, particularly those close to you.

What ways work best to teach children compassion?

9

DISASTER and EVIL

If the universe is so bad, or even half so bad, how on earth did human beings ever come to attribute it to the activity of a wise and good Creator? Men are fools, perhaps; but hardly so foolish as that. [Lewis, *Pain*, 15]

How often have you heard people say, "How can a loving God let that happen?" A bereaved parent cannot help but ask where God was when her child was killed. How often have you yourself wondered whether, considering the horrible things that happen throughout the world, God is in fact both all-loving and all-powerful?

The only "answer" possible—and to my mind the correct one—is in the book of Job. Job demands of God why one disaster after another should have happened to him, who has been "an upright man." God in effect dismisses the question as asked, responding simply that he, God, is the powerful creator of the world, while Job in comparison is a weak nothing.

Where were you when I laid the foundation of the earth?
Tell me, if you have understanding.
Who determined its measurements—surely you know!
Or who stretched the line upon it?
On what were its bases sunk,
or who laid its cornerstone,
when the morning stars sang together,
and all the sons of God shouted for joy? [Job 38:4-7]

God tells Job straight out that he, Job, is *unable* to understand. Out of the whirlwind, God's first words are, "Who is this that darkens counsel by words without knowledge?" [Job 38:2] Job, finally completely cowed, responds that he has "uttered what I did not understand, things too wonderful for me, which I did not know." [Job 42:3] And somehow or other, Job comes to an understanding not founded in reason but apparently fully acceptable to him. He says, "I had heard of thee by the hearing of the ear, but now my eye sees thee; therefore I despise myself, and repent in dust and ashes." [Job 42:5-6] Presumably, Job is repenting for his presumption, but the point here is that he considers himself answered.

While Jesus does not answer our question as to why a loving God permits disasters, he does in his parables make clear that the ways of God are not our ways and we need not, indeed *cannot*, understand everything. Remember the parable of the householder who hired laborers for his vineyard at different times during the day and then paid them all the same amount at the end of the day? If you read the parable carefully, you will see that Jesus is not saying that we should do the same thing, that the householder was being, in our view, "fair." The parable begins not by telling us to do as the householder did, but informing us that God in his kingdom is like the householder. It begins with these words: "The kingdom of heaven is like a householder who…" When the justice of the householder's equal payment to all is questioned by those who have worked longest, the householder responds, "Take what belongs to you, and go; I choose to give to this last as I give to you. Am I not allowed to do what I choose with what belongs to me? Or do you begrudge my generosity?" Jesus follows with the terse comment, "So the last will be first and the first last." [Matt. 20: 14-16] He is warning us that we cannot understand and certainly not judge the ways of God.

To help me accept my own inability to understand, I personally use a very humble—but I think not disrespectful—analogy of the relationship of God to man inherent in the book of Job. I am thinking of a sort of equation: "A" is to "B" as "B" is to "C"—God is to man as man is to dog. Let's take my mid-size, strawberry blonde mutt, Sunny, to illustrate. She no more understands my actions in general and particularly in relation to her than I understand God's actions in general and in relation to me.

Consider these examples. I put Sunny on a leash with a training collar and demand that she sit, lie down, stay, wait, and obey various other commands to which she has learned to acquiesce but which must make absolutely no sense to her. She learns, however, that her life is a lot more pleasant if she obeys me. Sometimes I let her out into the fenced dog yard, where she cannot chase the skittering red squirrels or the neighbor's teasing cat. Her instincts tell her to run after these critters, so why is she not allowed to do so? Then one day I pop her into a car, where she squeals and runs around for every moment of the half-hour trip to the veterinarian, excited and perhaps somewhat frightened. When we arrive, the vet pinches up her skin and gives her shots, holds onto one leg at a time to cut her nails, and performs all sorts of other indignities on her. Sunny of course has no idea why the vet is doing such undoglike things. Meanwhile her mom, meaning me, just stands around and allows it. Other times, her god—again meaning me—feeds her, takes her on walks, pets her, and is a fine and appropriately loving divinity. One of these days, her god will probably have to end her life with another trip to the vet.

Does Sunny understand all this? Not a bit. Sometimes she looks at me as if she is trying to figure it all out, but I am probably just anthropomorphizing. Despite my—to her—incomprehensible actions, she seems to accept me as her loving deity and still turns to me to meet her needs. She doesn't like what I do sometimes and the decisions I make, but I am the power in her life. I think that her response to me is the one I should have to God in times of misfortune or disaster. Not easy.

If we have trouble understanding the ills that befall ourselves, that is as nothing when we try to comprehend those that happen to others. We may figure out the cause and effect of some of our own unwise or selfish actions, and we may even come to perceive how certain chance occurrences fall within the will of God for us. However, when we ask why our friend should have had to face some difficulty, we are usually helpless to discern God's intent. In such circumstances, I am forcibly reminded of an incident in *The Horse and His Boy*, one of the Narnia children's books by C. S. Lewis. Aslan, the lion who is in this tale analogous with God, is answering the questions of a mare called Aravis, explaining that the scratches and bites that she received from unidentified lions were really from him, to let her know the pain that she had herself caused another. When Aravis accepts this and then asks a further question about this other, the Lion replies, "I am telling you your story, not hers. No-one is told any story but their own." [Lewis, *Horse*, 171] Much as we would like to know the story of those we love, why this and that have happened to them, what were God's purposes, we cannot. We are fortunate just to get a glimpse of his purposes for us.

The difficulty we feel in reconciling misfortunes and disasters with a god of love is the reason we need faith in its meaning as trust, the reason why a "leap of faith" is necessary. Without that leap, we cannot really trust that the Mystery that caused and continues to cause or at least to allow disasters is the same Spirit of love we sometimes experience and which makes for a fulfilling life. Jesus, and other people in whom the Spirit was strong, sensed, intuited, felt, somehow *knew* that, despite all the horrible events in the world, the creator and sustainer of the universe was one and the same with the powerful Spirit they experienced. And further, that the Spirit was unfailingly loving, one in which they could put their trust, despite what seemed like evidence to the contrary. They risked and sometimes surrendered their lives because their faith was so strong. If one thinks that Jesus's physical body as well as his spirit did in fact reappear after his death, then one can have even more trust in the union of the creator of this often dangerous universe with ultimate and unfailing love.

Not all theologians have accepted the problematical idea that the God of love is also the creator and sustainer of the universe. The latest and most notable example is Bishop Spong, who calls himself a "believer in exile." In his discussion of Christian creeds, he finds the term Almighty "troubling," pointing out that by "attributing omnipotence to God, one also attributes to the deity the power to remedy any wrong or to prevent any disaster. Yet wrongs and disasters continue to be a part of life." [Spong, 6] He puts the problem succinctly, but then in a few pages asks, "Could anyone worship a God dismissed as impotent?" He does not of course solve the intellectual problem. Hart faces the situation more squarely, saying "God, as creator, stands at the source of the reality in which we live, and to that extent is responsible for everything." [Hart, 130]

The most emotionally satisfying writing about this problem that I know is an essay by Annie Dillard. Describing in lurid detail horrible suffering by several good men, she questions in sharp words the presence and acquiescence of God in the face of disaster and evil. She alludes to others who have struggled with the problem, notably Pierre Teilhard de Chardin, who tried to reconcile original sin with his concept of evolution. She finally concludes: "I don't know. I don't know beans about God." [Dillard, 86] I know what she means, and I think Job surely did also.

Natural disasters are one thing. Evil in human beings is another. When an earthquake destroys a village, we react with horror, but somehow we can manage to accept the fact of natural disaster. However, when a person tortures another human being, our horror is strongly tinged with a gut feeling of disgust and an almost overpowering wish not to believe it did or could occur. There *is* a difference.

The connection between natural disasters and evil is hinted at in the last quotation given here from Job. After his revelation, when he says that he now sees as well as hears God, he follows with what seems like a non sequitur. He says, "Therefore I despise myself, and repent in dust and ashes." We ask why he should be repenting. We think that he had every right, as do we, to question God's actions when he cannot understand them. I think every reader of the book of Job is cheering him along, mentally saying, "Yes, God, explain yourself for once! Why did you let all those horrible things happen to this good man?" But Job, once he has "seen" God, begins to "despise" himself and to "repent." It is clear that he is repenting not for past sins that might in the eyes of some have been the cause of all his misfortunes, but for what he now understands as his arrogance in questioning God. In theological language, the sin of pride.

Two questions arise immediately when considering sin and evil, the latter term as used here meaning sin in its extreme form. One is: Why does God allow men to be evil? This introduces the subject of free will, without which we speculate that all would be well—though of course unimaginably dull—between man and man as well as man and God. God allows us to go our own way, and we hurt each other and ourselves. The other question is: Why, having free will, do we so often choose to sin? This leads to defining what sin is and how we can avoid it, since it obviously produces unhappiness all around.

Harking back to Job, we know that no "why" questions have clear and completely satisfactory answers, so once again we have the response that we can't know and don't in fact need to know the reason the universe was created as it was in order for us to come into harmony with the Mystery/Spirit/Creator of that universe. However, accepting that we cannot understand the "why" of the creation, we can nevertheless find analogies within the universe that may help us conceive of a God who is both all-loving and all-powerful, even though he has given his creatures a seemingly unlimited ability to harm themselves and others.

The analogy that seems most apt to me pictures God as a chess wizard. Here it is in fable form (with apologies to Rudyard Kipling).

◆   ◆   ◆

THE CHESS WIZARD. Once upon a time—really "once *before* a time"—there was a mighty and eternal wizard who loved nothing better than playing chess, and his skill at the game knew no bounds. However, no matter how hard he tried, he could not induce the beasts of the field, the birds in the air, or the fish in the sea to play chess with him. They excused themselves, saying, "We are too busy eating, sleeping, and reproducing to bother with any old chess game."

Being a wizard as he was, and a mighty one at that, he was not to be hindered from indulging his love of chess by a host of beasts, birds, and fish. So he thought for a moment, and then with a big smile he waved his wizard wand from left to right, and right to left many times, and—lo and behold—table after table of chess players appeared before him, stretching into the distance as far as the eye could see. And before each one lay a chessboard and all the pieces, with the moves clearly written out on a pad of paper beside them.

The wizard then spoke to the multitude of chess players before him. (Being a mighty wizard, he had a mighty voice, which could be heard throughout the hall.) He spoke thus: "I will play a game of chess with each one of you, and you will play games with each other. However, the games with each other are only practice. The game with me is the one that counts. You have before you information on the way each piece moves, but you yourselves must each figure out how to win. Let the games begin!" And they did.

Now you must understand that the wizard was no ordinary chess player. He was able to see aeons ahead, gauge all variables, and comprehend the possible interactions of all players with each other. Old players died and new ones were born, and still the games continued. For a long while, these multitudinous chess contests amused the wizard, but eventually he longed to see a few more winners at his tables. Despite the shelves of books on game strategy that they had written, very few players had discovered how to win consistently.

Finally, the wizard decided to create a special player able to perceive the secret of winning and to tell the others. To do this, he picked up the wand that the players always termed "chance," because they did not want to believe that the wizard had any interest or control beyond setting up the games at the beginning, determining the rules, and playing according to those rules. With this wand of "chance," the wizard carefully picked out the precise new player that he wished from the trillions and even zillions of possible new players, and let him be born at the exact moment when his skill in the game would be noticed.

As planned, this new player attracted immediate and lasting attention, largely because, although he disobeyed almost all the strategies for winning that were laid down in all the books men had written on chess, he seemed to be winning the one with the wizard. In fact, he lost all the matches with his fellow players, one after another. This did not disturb him, however, because he knew that he had discovered the secret of winning the important game, the one with the wizard. And he did win. At that the wizard smiled, because he himself at last had lost. (Or had he thereby won?)

So, did the other players learn from that one successful player the secret of winning? In a way, yes, because the secret became common knowledge, but according to the wizard's log book, there have still not been many winners. The players' urge to win each little game with each other is just so strong that they seem to forget the secret: That only by being willing to lose the little games can they win the big one. And so the games continue.

◆   ◆   ◆

The point is that, even as the chess wizard by using chance and his overarching omniscience and wisdom could make life work out well in his sight if not in that of the players, so perhaps can God-Mystery-Creator-Spirit do in our lives. In spite of, but also partially through, our free will.

The fable also says something about why we chess players do not more often win the primary game with the wizard and our games with each other. Our first "mistake" is forgetting that the only game that counts is the one with the wizard and our second mistake is wanting to win *over* each other. We are reminded of Jesus's response to the Pharisees' question concerning the "great commandment" in the law. He said: "You shall love the Lord your God with all your heart, and with all your soul, and with all your mind. This is the great and first commandment. And a second is like it, You shall love your neighbor as yourself. On these two commandments depend all the laws and the prophets." [Matt 22:37-40] In the fable, the "new player" who was successful is of course Jesus. Like most analogies, the fable cannot be pressed too far.

So, even though we must accept that we cannot understand why man does not naturally love God and his fellowman, most of us nevertheless learn eventually, simply through living, that happiness is a condition of the spirit more than of the mind and body. Recognizing that fact, we have available to us the teachings of Jesus and other sages, as well as the examples of many people around us, that only through loving others—through being compassionate toward them—can we ourselves find happiness.

Why does God allow disasters and evil? How can it be that an all-loving God, if he is all-powerful, does not do something about it? Once again, we find that we know all we need to know. Difficult as the subjects of disaster and evil are to our minds and hearts, we are not lacking the tools we need to deal with them in our lives. Wendell Berry, a contemporary poet and novelist, capsulizes the situation in a deeply felt exclamation: "Within limits we can know. Within somewhat wider limits we can imagine. We can extend compassion to the limit of imagination. We can love, it seems, beyond imagining. But how little we can understand!" [Berry, *World*, 149]

We must, like Job, humbly and realistically confess that as humans we simply cannot understand. We might consider Albert Einstein's description of his religion as consisting of "a humble admiration of the illimitable superior spirit who reveals himself in the slight details we are able to perceive with our frail and feeble mind." [quoted by Hart, 7] And then we must turn our backs on the why and move forward, dedicating ourselves to living lives of compassion and love in harmony with the Mystery of the universe.

◆   ◆   ◆

If we accept with Job that God is the lord of all creation and that we mortals cannot possibly understand his ways, many of which seem contradictory to us, what is our reaction? Throughout the ages, humankind has reacted to his awareness of God's power and his own weakness with worship. We have bowed down before the power of the universe. So let us turn now to the subject of worship.

DISCUSSION QUESTIONS

Do you side with Job in the Book of Job? Have you ever railed against God, or the powers that be? Do you think that addressing God as Job does is okay?

Are you willing to accept your inability to reconcile the love of God with the disasters and evil in the world? Or have you a way of doing so that you find satisfactory?

Do you find the analogy of human to God with dog to human meaningful? Or is it somehow disrespectful, simplistic, and/or disturbing?

Is the fable of the chess wizard helpful to you in considering the issue of free will and an all-powerful God?

10

GLORY and WORSHIP

When we've been there ten thousand years, bright shining as the
sun,
We've no less days to sing God's praise than when we'd first begun.
[John Newton, *Amazing Grace, 1779*]

I have always been puzzled by the frequent exhortations in the Bible
and in Christian liturgy to "glorify God," to "give God glory." To me,
this seems presumptuous indeed. Surely God, the creator of the universe, is already glorious and does not need to be made so by his creatures, as in "glorify." Nor does he need to be "given glory," which I
assume means praise. Certainly he does not hanker after praise from us.
So why are we told again and again that we should glorify God who is
already glorious and praise him who needs no praise?

Obviously, I have been bumping into a definition problem. The
most helpful dictionary definition for "glorify," not the first, is "give
worshipful praise, honor, and thanksgiving to." The key word is "worshipful." Most of us naturally, although usually only figuratively, bow
down in submission or yield to someone whom we recognize as more
powerful than we are. That reaction is only common sense, a safety
measure.

Throughout nature, the weak submit to the strong or pay the price,
as do those so-termed "heroes" in Greek and Roman mythology, who
defied the supreme power of the gods. The animal world is full of
examples and, I suspect, few or no exceptions. Consider our dogs in
relation to us, echoing the parallel relationship I pointed to in the last
chapter. A dog, upon meeting a person (or sometimes another dog)

whom he recognizes as clearly very dominant, will often crouch and flatten his ears, sometimes in fact rolling over and exposing his stomach. Each animal species has its own way of acknowledging the dominance of another. People have had the same self-preserving instinct from earliest times, when primitive man bowed down and tried to appease the threatening and frightening forces of nature. In medieval times, peasants and knights bowed and scraped before their kings. And for centuries people of all religious faiths have expressed their subservience by both bowing down and kneeling before their god. It is an instinctive reaction in the presence of superior power.

The problem for people, however, is that many of us live our lives foolishly unaware that we *are* in the presence of a superior power. We feel that we are for the most part doing just fine without God, until we find ourselves in that proverbial foxhole where no man is an atheist. As a species, we have been discovering the laws of nature and learning to use and control the earth. We even aspire to doing so with the entire universe, given enough time. Only a small number of us are becoming aware that in our pride and heedlessness, we may be shortening the time available for us as a species upon this planet.

The human tendency to feel powerful in our own right is not new: hence the exhortations in all religions to remember our powerlessness before the creator of the universe and to do what comes naturally—bow down, acknowledging our dependence. We are to do this not because God demands it, but because it is the natural and instinctive thing to do if we view the world realistically, not hiding our heads in the sand while the hurricanes rage above us.

When we look up and around, we cannot but consider that creation of which we are a part. Then we not only are in awe of the creation, but we praise the creator, because the more we learn about the earth and the universe, the more wonderful they seem to us, from the tiniest parts to the largest. With few exceptions, when we move from our mundane, here-and-now concerns, and take the time to think seriously about the creation, we are filled with wonder. All we need to do is consider a small part of the whole, for example birds, with their infinite differences, migration habits, and beauty. And then comes praise for whoever or whatever caused all this to be. I could here quote endlessly the words of poets, scientists, theologians, and others. Let me just give two that I happen to have run into recently. Martin Luther, quoted by Kathleen Norris, wrote that "if you understand a single grain of wheat you would die of wonder." [Norris, 245] Similarly, Thomas Hart, pointing out that "wonder is the basis of worship," notes that "almost anything might put us in awe if we are really present to it." [Hart, 101]

When we find ourselves living in this beautiful world, this astoundingly interesting, vital, and endless universe, thankfulness comes, again naturally. Thankfulness to whoever or whatever placed us here, thankfulness to the power or powers that be, before whom we are as nothing. We have bowed down before the power, we have praised in wonder at the beauty and vitality, and finally we become thankful in acknowledgment of our having been made a part of such a world. We have experienced the three major elements of worship—submission, praise, and thankfulness.

However, an important ingredient of the thankfulness of those spiritually aware has not yet been mentioned. Not only have we been lucky enough to be alive and part of this creation, but the God who made us communicates with us human beings in love, no matter how vainglorious and foolish we may often be. We may refuse to acknowledge him as creator, we may think we are self-sufficient and completely independent, and we may act in pride and willfulness toward him and our fellow human beings, and yet somehow he forgives us and offers his Spirit of love to us. He is the Eternal Now, always there for us. Those who have been and are aware of this love, Christians and non-Christians alike, thank God not only for being a part of his creation but for his mercy in deigning to sustain us and for his love in offering us the fulfillment we crave.

And so we worship our God—the Mystery, the Spirit—in acknowledgment and submission to his power, in praise of his creation, and in thankfulness for his love and mercy. This, I have come to think, is what is meant by "glorifying" God. The phrase still needs translation for my modern ear, but the naturalness of the responses to the creator makes it understandable to me.

So how do we respond in worship? Remember my dog parallel? How does my dog Sunny respond when I, her mistress, approach, this mistress who controls her life, feeds her, pets her, walks with her, and talks gently to her? She jumps for joy, turns circles, licks my hand, and expresses her joy in all the ways available to her. This is her worship. May we do as well.

Worship is the way we express a natural and appropriate relationship to the Mystery surrounding us. The stronger our awareness of this relationship, the more urgency we feel to express it in whatever way we can. The drive to express one or more of the elements of worship has led to many forms of art. The form most often associated with worship is music, in which the composer or performer revels in the relationships of sounds to each other, their ability to express his emotions and aspirations, the way rhythm corresponds to the natural motions of the human body. The musician may or may not be producing a frankly "religious" piece. He is, however, at the least turning into art his reactions to those aspects of the creation to which he is most attuned. The extraordinary power of music to express emotion was put this way by Wes Blomster, a music critic at the Boston Globe: "We would like to think that in life's most exalted moments, when the boundaries of language restrict us in the expression of our feelings, it's music that takes over and says the unsayable." This comment was made in his review of the final concert directed by Rostopovich with the National Symphony Orchestra.

Painters and sculptors also revel in relationships, not of sounds but of lines and forms to each other, the way they give body to their yearnings and joys, and above all the beauty of the natural world. This is true not only of the artists who have created the frankly "religious" art that we see in places of worship, but equally of those who produce still-life, portraits, or abstract works.

The worship in poetry is perhaps most obvious to those of us for whom language rather than music and art communicates most clearly. We enjoy the sounds of words, the interrelationships of ideas, the possibilities of syntax and rhythms in addition to the satisfaction of expressing our strongest feelings and convictions. I am thinking now not only of the poets who write about the holiness of God and the beauties and powers of the world, but particularly of the many who transmit a sense of the mystery inherent in all of life and of the yearning for union with the spiritual reality that underlies it. Poet Kathleen Norris writes that "poetry, like prayer, tends to be a dialogue with the holy." [Norris, 379]

Worshipful creativity is not limited to "artists." The poet Kathleen Norris notes that "both science and poetry reveal the mysterious connections that undergird our lives, and the religious sensibility knows its truth." [Norris, 288] Most of us do not have the talents to worship by composing music, painting pictures, and writing poetry. We nevertheless may acknowledge our dependence on God, admire his creation, and be thankful that we are a part of it. What is *our* natural way to worship? Here I return to my theme of diversity, of how different we all are. Remember my dog Sunny, dancing circles of joy, often at the mere thought of a walk with me? How easy it is for her to show her worship of her mistress and her delight in our relationship. Our other, older dog used to merely wag her tail and rise expectantly when my husband, the person *she* worshiped, proffered a walk. Even in the canine species, there are differences.

There is a lot of worshiping going on by many of us that is never named as such. People who enjoy working in their particular occupation and do so in awareness that they are part of God's creation dealing with other wonderful parts of that creation (whether animal, vegetable, or mineral) may be involved in worship of a kind. They know their place in the universe, they marvel at what they are dealing with (even when it is with difficult people), and they are happy to be alive.

I have just been reading Jane Smiley's novel, *Horse Heaven,* about people and horses in the horse racing industry, none of whom would be called religious or worshipful in the ordinary sense. And yet there is a lot of worshiping occurring, primarily in response to the beauty, vitality, strength, and personality of various horses. Many of the characters express wonder and awe at these animals, and some are thankful to be associated with them. The element of worship that is missing, however, in some of the characters is awareness that they are dependent on whatever is out there running it all, i.e., the Mystery. And yet in some instances this dependence is felt in response to the high level of uncertainty and risk inherent in horse racing, which leads to expressions such as, "better lucky than good" and "that's horses." A few of the owners and trainers feel that they are so clever and intuitive that all successes must be credited to them and all failures and accidents are the responsibility of their colleagues or themselves. These persons are obviously in no sense worshiping. But those who are aware of their dependence on fate, luck, or something out there, who are continually in awe at the splendor of the horse, and who are thrilled to be working with such an animal, are really experiencing an unconscious but nevertheless real type of worship at the moments of their awareness.

Many of us have such moments, felt primarily as thankfulness. I have heard many not-very-healthy elders remark, with a grin, that if they can just wake up in the morning, get out of bed, and look forward to something they have to do, they are happy enough. Morning worship, whether or not a prayer of words is uttered. An audience, at the conclusion of an outstanding performance of a beautiful piece of music, ofttimes will be silent for a moment before breaking out in applause. They have had an emotional and spiritual experience of something beyond the world of the senses, they wonder at the beauty of what they have heard, and they are thankful to have been present at this moment, when this piece was performed by these performers.

Again, this qualifies as a moment of worship, including both the silence and the release of applause as a natural expression.

A more homely example from my own daily life can perhaps be easily translated into that of any reader. As has undoubtedly been clear from the foregoing chapters, I am an "animal lover." I was about to write, "particularly horses," but then I thought, "no, I love dogs just as much." This was followed by, "but I would miss having a cat." So much for that. The example that came to mind was about horses. As a child, I was thrilled by the opportunity of riding for a few months at a summer camp, but my parents would not yield to my desire to learn to ride horseback in our home town. Then came college, marriage, and children. When my oldest child began riding lessons with the Girl Scouts, I found my opportunity and began lessons myself at the age of thirty-four. After many lessons, I finally owned a horse—in fact two horses—stabled at a friend's place and then at commercial stables. I had the excitement of riding to the hounds and the adventure of trail riding. When my husband and I moved north to central Massachusetts, I at last was able to keep my horses on our own property. Now I not only ride them, but delight in taking care of them and in simply looking out at the pasture and seeing those beautiful creatures out there. I have the opportunity to see them close up day to day, to feed them, stroke them, talk to them, and to know that they are mine—insofar as any living creature can be said to belong to another. I am thrilled by their beauty, enthralled by their "horsiness," and filled with thankfulness many times a day. These moments are small worship times for me, not of the horses of course, but of the Mystery out there who has granted me such a gift. Those to whom horses, dogs, and cats are not important can easily substitute a child, a mate, a place, a sport. It is still worship if awareness of dependence, praise, and thankfulness are in their hearts.

◆   ◆   ◆

So far, we have been considering solo worship, which is not what generally comes to mind when one speaks of "worship." Appropriately so. We are herd animals, pack animals, group animals, despite the attempts many of us make to go it alone. Most of our pleasures are increased when they are shared with someone else of our own species. (Even I, as an avowed animal lover, usually wish for a human companion to share my enjoyment of animals.) We instinctively run to share with others our good fortune, our excitement, our fun. Likewise, apparently from the beginning of time, we humans have had an instinct and a yearning to worship with others as well as by ourselves. Group worship, worship in a community, is the topic of the next chapter.

DISCUSSION QUESTIONS

Has the injunction to "glorify God" ever puzzled you as it has me?

What part of nature most fills you with awe and wonder?

Does the idea of expressing submission bother you, or does it come naturally?

How do you most naturally express submission, praise, and thankfulness? Is it by creating or participating in music, art, or poetry, or in some other way?

Do you worship in a way that is not usually termed "worship"? How?

11

CHURCH and COMMUNITY

Heaven is a city and not a solitude. [John of Patmos, quoted by Norris, 383]

How often I have heard people, young and old, insist that they "believe in God" but admit that they neither belong to a religious group nor attend worship services. They consider themselves religious but, as one woman put it to me, correctly certain that I would understand her meaning, not "too religious." Can we be religious in the sense of living a fulfilling spiritual life without participating in group worship? And if we can, what has group worship to offer us that is sufficiently rewarding to compensate for the hour plus travel time lost from other activities?

Before extolling the various values of participating in group worship—which I shall do in a moment—I must admit that my own church attendance during the last twenty years or so has been sporadic. The primary reason that I personally attend a Sunday church service is to remind myself of "true north," to put myself into a community where everyone acknowledges that God is all-loving, all-powerful, and the only source of happiness. I am trying to counteract the effects of a largely secular society on my approach to life. My secondary reason is that I think the church, being ideally a group of people publicly dedicated to doing God's will, is a potentially powerful instrument of God in our world, fully deserving of my support, both through donation of money (no problem) and through attendance (more of a problem). I

107

am still working on making real to myself the values of group worship that I have read about and observed in other people.

It may be that I shall not succeed in that endeavor. In group worship particularly, what fits one does not fit all. I suspect that finding the particular congregation whose worship is most meaningful to oneself as an individual is at least part of the key, with learning to adapt perhaps being the remaining part.

Let us begin by considering the nature of group worship. Poet Kathleen Norris speaks of "the mystery of worship, which is God's presence and our response to it." [Norris, 72] She writes that "we praise God not to celebrate our own faith but to give thanks for the faith God has in us. To let ourselves look at God, and let God look back at us. And to laugh, and sing, and be delighted because God has called us his own." [Norris, 151] Can we not do that all by ourselves? Yes, we can. But do we do it better or more completely by doing it with others? I suspect we do, or at least many people do.

This past winter, I read three books by current writers struggling to regain or renew their Christian faith in the context of intimate participation in Christian congregations. Kathleen Norris, in *Amazing Grace: A Vocabulary of Faith*, deals chapter by chapter with what she calls "the vocabulary of the Christian church," which seemed "dauntingly abstract to me, even vaguely threatening." [Norris, 2] She wanted the words to become real "in an existential sense." [Norris, 3] To this end, she attended a Benedictine monastery, which became the subject of an earlier book entitled *The Cloister Walk*, and then she worked with various churches where she sought out, and seems to have found to her own satisfaction, the meaning of the "scary" words she deals with in her book in a partly theological, partly memoir fashion.

Nora Gallagher in many ways writes of a similar journey in *Things Seen and Unseen: A Year Lived in Faith*. Her book is organized by the seasons of the Christian calendar, which take her through a year of active participation in an Episcopal church in Santa Barbara, California. As with Norris, the church she attended played a major part in her spiritual journey.

Novelist Anne Lamott, in *Traveling Mercies: Some Thoughts on Faith,* also presents a highly personal account of her coming to religious faith and mature spirituality, but she does it more in the form of a memoir in which a Presbyterian church in Marin City, California, is a propelling force.

All three authors believe that the Christian congregations of which they were a part, in both their worship services and their various ways of ministering to others, were crucial to their attainment of a living faith. The authors' witness will be seen many times below, along with that of other writers on the subject. While all three women's experiences were in relation to Christian congregations, they could well have been with congregations of other faiths. I would ask the reader to remember this fact and make the translation necessary, when I use the word "church," to designate all congregations of various religious convictions.

The special offerings of the church may be roughly categorized as (1) doctrine or tradition, consisting usually of a system of intellectual beliefs handed down and taught over the centuries; (2) liturgy, ritual, and ceremony, meaning a regular way of combining the various elements of group worship, such as anthems, hymns, scriptures, sermon, and prayers; and (3) community, referring to the group itself as it worships together, supports and socializes with its own members, and acts as one in the larger community to give a practical form to its shared faith.

Most of us do not want to be told what to believe. The idea of doctrine is not appealing at all to our modern, skeptical minds, and I suspect that among the people joining a congregation on a particular Sunday morning there are at least a few who, while giving all the positive answers required by the service for new members, secretly harbor doubts about certain statements of belief therein. And so they should. Doctrine is not what we should or must believe in order to join with others in the worship of God. It is, rather, a statement of what others in a particular religious faith have come to perceive as truth. Henri Nouwen puts it this way: "Doctrines are not alien formulations which we must adhere to but the documentation of the most profound human experiences which, transcending time and place, are handed over from generation to generation as a light in our darkness." [Nouwen, 89]

A system of beliefs is just that—an intellectual formulation of the meaning of the spiritual experiences of a very large number of people. Kathleen Norris writes that "dogmas represent what is basically agreed on as the foundation of the faith." [Norris, 324] They tell us what other people have concluded. Norris again: "Faith simply is, and what the religious traditions of the world do is to give us guidance as to how to interpret our own experience in the light of what our ancestors have made of it over the centuries." [Norris, 103]

So what is the spiritual value to us of the systems of belief handed down for our use? In a word, they make us think and consider. Insofar as we value the wisdom of our elders, of those who have "been there," we will at least consider seriously their carefully thought-out formulations about their faith. We will try to imagine what experiences led them to a particular statement or conclusion. We will try to translate their words and phrases into language that is meaningful to us in our own lives. We will *not* just toss off what may seem like a weird idea without at least attempting to find the life behind it.

For example, we will not say, "What in the world is the Holy Ghost? Ghosts!" Or perhaps, "The Trinity? I thought this was a religion of one God." And, "How about the Calvinist idea of predestination? Makes no sense if we have free will!" If we are serious about spiritual matters, we will resist the youthful urge to toss out the wisdom of our elders because it is not phrased in today's language, and instead we will take a careful look at what they were trying to express.

On the other hand, we must not simply try to swallow it all whole in our attempt to be part of a particular religious denomination or congregation. As usual, the middle ground is best: neither throw it out nor blindly accept every word, but use it as a tool for spiritual growth. Marcus Borg, using the word "tradition" to include doctrine, writes of both its dangers and value: "[W]hen tradition is thought to state the way things really are, it becomes the director and judge of our lives; we are, in effect, imprisoned by it. On the other hand, tradition can be understood as a pointer to that which is beyond tradition: the sacred. Then it functions not as a prison but as a lens." [Borg, *God*, 100]

As our thoughts about our spiritual experiences grow, our theology develops, but it must remain "an adjunct and response to a lived faith." [Norris, 259] In my chapter on belief and faith, I noted the danger of letting theology harden, and it is a point worth repeating to those of us with analytical minds. We must never conclude that we "have it all figured out." Such a hardening stunts our own spiritual growth as well as leading to a self-righteous type of evangelism. As Hart reminds us, "spirituality remains religion's vital core. It challenges, expands, and reforms organized religion. The relationship is reciprocal, dynamic, mutually enriching." [Hart, 47] Nouwen says that it "demands the continuing refusal to identify God with any concept, theory, document or event, thus preventing man or woman from becoming a fanatic sectarian or enthusiast, while allowing for an ongoing growth in gentleness and receptivity." [Nouwen, 105] In other words, doctrine and tradition are indeed useful if we use them "not as a prison but as a lens."

What I name as the second offering of the church may be equally problematic and indeed become a barrier more formidable than doctrine. Ritual, liturgy, and sacrament. All bring to mind ceremonies and procedures that, if not familiar from childhood, are likely to seem foreign, incomprehensible, disconcerting at the least. Yet they all serve the same purpose—to make the presence of the Eternal Spirit real to us, which is the often unrecognized but inescapable desire of human beings.

Thomas Hart calls ritual "the expression in symbolic action of realities beyond words." [Hart, 164] Liturgy, literally "the work of the people," consists of the words that over the ages have seemed most helpful in making human beings aware of the presence of God, the Mystery, the Eternal Spirit. Marcus Borg defines a sacrament as "a practice that makes the sacred mystery accessible." He explains that the original Latin word translated the Greek word for "mystery" (referring to "sacred mystery") and meant any spiritually symbolic object or practice with a sacred character or function. [Borg, *God*, 115]

I return yet again to the theme of how different we all are. These differences have led to a multitude of ways to worship. There is the silence and personal witness of the Quakers, the planned and often revised "modern" services of most Protestants, the "joyful noise" and hallelujahs for still other more free-wheeling and expressive groups, and the ornate ceremonies and ancient rituals of the Greek and Roman Catholics. Kathleen Norris expresses some amusement at the differences, writing that "in worship, disparate people seek a unity far greater than the sum of themselves but don't have much control over how, or if, this happens. Recklessly, we let loose with music, and the words of hymns, the psalms, canticle, and prayers." [Norris, 246] Add to these Christian practices the ways in which Buddhists, Hindus, Muslims, and all other religious groups have chosen to express their worship, and you have a wide choice! All, as Borg notes, are "part of secondhand religion. Yet their spiritual function is to mediate firsthand religious experience: to bring about an opening of the heart to the reality of the sacred all around us." [Borg, *God*, 122]

How ritual accomplishes this "opening of the heart" is unclear, but we do know that it gives rise to a deeply felt response in many people. C. S. Lewis remarked that people who have deserted their churches often say that the ritual is what they miss the most. Ritual "can shape the religious imagination." [Borg, *God*, 117] But silence also is valuable, in that it "invites us into a wordless world. It also conveys the sense that something is present that is worth attending to." [Borg, *God*,

119] In his enthusiasm for the effectiveness of ritual, Borg plays down the function of a sermon or meditation as "perhaps the least effective way of reaching the heart," because "the spoken word tends to go to our heads, not our hearts." [Borg, *God*, 122]

Marcus Borg suggests that the church building as well as the ritual contributes to our ability to sense the reality of the sacred all around and within us. He writes of the more ceremonial churches: "The internal space of the church building and what happens there—from the use of subdued light, holy icons, and elaborate vestments to the smoke and smell of incense and the sung liturgy—create a sense that we are temporarily entering another world.... when one enters this space, one enters a different reality." [Borg, *God*, 120] William James speaks of "richness" as the "supreme imaginative requirement" for some, including institutional complexity. [James, 358] Such a person, he says, has a "monarchial imagination" and when in an architecturally beautiful church with elaborate ritual "feels then as if in presence of some vast incrusted work of jewelry or architecture." [James, 358]

Those of us who were not brought up in an elaborate church with a set liturgy and perhaps accompanying ceremony may find it difficult not to be distracted in a setting that has both, and we may be unable to respond appropriately. We all tend to like what is familiar. C. S. Lewis remarked, within a defense of an established and unmodified liturgy, that "the prayers to which I can most fully attend in church are always those I have most often used in my bedroom." [Lewis, *Prayer,* 100] Such prayers do not require the attempt to understand and perhaps critique their theology, thus freeing the heart. In these days, however, the many people who were not part of a church community as children seem to eschew liturgy and ceremony in favor of what they feel is plain, everyday, and therefore understandable language. The question is whether or not such language can "bring about an opening of the heart to the reality of the sacred all around us." [Borg, *God*, 122] Unfortunately, the prayers of many churches are in effect sermonettes, small theological essays, directed primarily to our intellects.

Poet Kathleen Norris, while having found many Christian terms "scary," was enthralled by the language and rituals of the Benedictine monastery where she spent some weeks. She found them much more effective than the trendy, often psychological language of many modern congregations. She writes that "modern believers tend to trust in therapy more than in mystery, a fact that tends to manifest itself in worship that employs the bland speech of pop psychology and self-help rather than language resonant with poetic meaning." [Norris, 71] This language to her does not resonate with the mystery of the Eternal Spirit. "[T]o my ear, such language reflects an idolatry of ourselves, that is, the notion that the measure of what we can understand, what is readily comprehensible and acceptable to us, is also the measure of God." [Norris, 72] She is reacting to the secular nature of our society.

Robert Coles, a research psychologist working in various functions at Harvard University, discusses idolatry of the self in some detail in a recent book about the development of what he terms "the secular mind." He points out that it indeed *has* "faith," not in a religion, but in science and more basically "in ourselves, in our ability to know ourselves, gain control of things (with and outside ourselves) through such knowledge. And increasingly these recent years,…in the capacity of the human brain…to explore itself, understand itself fully, gain operating (clinical) control over its vulnerabilities, aberrancies." [Coles, 116] In other words, worship of the self as savior of the self.

It may be that the use of modern language, even though tainted with our human theories, does bring a religious element into our usually secular way of thinking about ourselves and our lives—which of course is not an appeal to the heart nor does it bring a sense of the sacredness within life. However, I think it is attractive to many people who are "trying out" the church for some reason—be it to become part of a community, because they think their children should be at least "exposed" to religion in a Sunday School, or perhaps because of a half-acknowledged sense that something is missing from their lives. They are among the many who are experiencing what the Dalai Lama terms "a neglect of...our inner dimension." [DL, 16] They feel more "comfortable" with modern language.

Often young people who have left the church, proud of the skeptical intellectual approach typical of their age and times, will almost in spite of themselves turn back to it at least briefly in order to observe the tradition of infant baptism. "The grandparents would be so pleased." Baptism is a time to gather the family around to marvel at the new baby, regardless of religious belief or commitment. And then some of the parents begin to wonder. They hear the words of the sacrament of infant baptism, and perhaps they are moved. They ask themselves if there is really anything in this? They may remember their own early Sunday School days with a certain pleasure, or realize that if they hadn't gone to Sunday School they would not have learned anything at all about the Bible. Soon they are asking each other, "Should we make the effort to take our child to Sunday School?"

One of the parents may come up with the not unusual and supposedly "broadminded" theory that children should be allowed to choose their own religion, if any, when they are old enough to do so. That is something like saying that you shouldn't teach French to your young son who is destined to move to France; that when he moves to France—that will be early enough. Only parents who intend that the child *not* go to France and who themselves know nothing of France or the French language, would be so foolish. A child needs to be introduced to the spiritual world, to learn its "language." The earlier, the better. He needs to become aware of the spiritual aspect of his own life and to see it exemplified in other people. It is conceivable that a child's parents are sufficiently spiritual themselves so that they can teach their child the language, much as one could teach a child French by speaking it occasionally at home. But this approach is obviously far inferior to letting the child learn French where French is spoken.

Usually a child is withheld from Sunday School because the parents are so immersed in our secular society that they are neglecting any spiritual life they may have known earlier. The best Sunday Schools, and probably in fact *most* Sunday Schools, let children know that to many people throughout the centuries God has been and still is very real; they tell them that they are loved by this God; they relate both stories and parables that underlie Western culture and that are not come by easily in any other way; and they expose them to the liturgy and ritual that can awaken them to the reality of the nonsecular world. A child who is not "exposed" to religion early is off to a poor start in becoming spiritually fulfilled.

While sacraments are part of the liturgy and ritual in many congregations, they stand apart and have been specifically designated as particularly effective ways of making the sacred accessible. Baptism and the Lord's Supper are examples. The discussions and divisive arguments throughout Christendom as to the exact meaning of both have abounded. In baptism, is immersion necessary? In the Lord's Supper, or Communion, does the bread and wine (or grape juice) actually become the body and blood of the crucified Jesus after it has been consecrated? More importantly, of course, what do they mean to you and me? I have discovered that even within modern Protestant congregations, each individual seems to have some way of gleaning significance from the sacraments. For me, the ordinariness of water, bread, and wine that are used in the sacraments is a focused reminder that all things in my everyday life are infused with the holy, that the Eternal Spirit is in all that I touch and see and hear and taste and experience, telling me that I am indeed cherished.

As noted earlier, although I have belonged to one Protestant church after another throughout my life, I am not a devotee of group worship in the sense that I always want very much to attend a Sunday service and miss it terribly or feel guilty if I do not. In fact, I am at the moment writing this chapter on a Sunday morning at home, having decided that writing was the best use of this particular time. While I have always been able to appreciate the value of tradition and doctrine, I admit that I do not respond fully to unfamiliar liturgy and ritual. I am able to understand and even empathize with what I read about their effectiveness in bringing a sense of the sacred, but I have not been able to experience it as forcefully as others obviously do. It may be that I could develop the ability with more exposure, but I suspect that, by nature and perhaps upbringing also, I will remain unable to fully appreciate most aspects of liturgy and ritual. I am happy that at least the music in a church service often gives me a special awareness of a deeper reality, and the sacraments, in particular the Lord's Supper, are very meaningful for me. We are all different. Fortunately, there is a wide choice of religious congregations from which to choose the one or perhaps two that most often and most completely mediate a sense of God's presence.

The third distinct offering of religious groups is community. As urban populations in industrialized nations have been increasing, the human need for more community living has been noted, described, explained, and preached. It is perceived either that too many of us live in little units apart from our fellowman, or that we are trying to survive cheek by jowl in a jumble of unknown and seemingly unknowable human creatures. Human beings are—we just *are*—herd animals, some of us more than others. Not only do we feel a need to be part of a group, we want to be part of a relatively small group where we are known for who we are. Such a group is called a community.

Ideally, religious congregations offer a community of people who worship God together, provide spiritual and emotional support for each other, and act together to do what they perceive as the will of God. Being part of a worshiping group adds a certain comfort, warmth, and even meaning to our participation in ritual, liturgy, and sacrament. We somehow sense that we are doing these things as we were meant to, in our herd. One can of course sing a hymn out in the meadows all by oneself and enjoy doing so. Even the most solitary person, however, is apt to admit that it just "ain't the same thing" as singing hymns with a lot of other enthusiastic people. Marcus Borg describes the experience of what he terms "participatory music": "Through it, one becomes part of a community and harmony of sacred sound. Moreover, the opportunity to 'sing one's heart out' is provided by accessible hymns that can be sung with enthusiasm. In hymns of praise, we often experience being drawn out of ourselves." [Borg, *God*, 118] Note that word "accessible." Borg, like C. S. Lewis, seems to prefer the familiar as an aid to worship.

Some congregations excel in providing community support. All three of the authors on whom I rely for much of this chapter were fortunate in finding such congregations, and then—equally important—entered into full participation with them. Nora Gallagher, who was not only active on the boards of her congregation but also volunteered in the Kitchen it sponsored, hints at the challenge of a close relationship with a wide variety of people: "In that little church, I began to understand 'the community of faith,' how, like your family, it presents you with people you would not normally choose." [N. Gallagher, 67] Norris is amusing on the subject of how one may feel about other members of a congregation: "I have come to suspect that when people complain about 'organized' religion what they are really saying is that they can't stand other people. At least not enough to trust them to help work out a 'personal' spirituality." [Norris, 258]

So here you have an assorted bunch of people, bound together by a desire to worship God, by a general belief that they should love each other and everyone else, and perhaps also by a neighborhood. Their lives may be completely different from yours in every possible way. You may have nothing in common with them except a desire to worship God in approximately the same way and to live in active love. In some congregations, those with dedicated people, that is sufficient to make a strong network of caring.

My home is located in a community with exactly such a congregation. All who live in the area qualify for support of a very practical nature, whether or not they profess a faith, belong to the congregation, or attend its functions. Importantly, while everyone is tacitly invited to join this congregation, there is no proselytizing. Norris writes well on this subject, saying that evangelism "means living in such a way that others may be attracted to you and your values, but not taking this as a license to preach to them about the strength and joy that you've found in knowing Jesus.... The best evangelism—the show, don't tell kind—presumes an understanding of relationship that precludes forcing your faith, and the language of that faith, on another person." [Norris, 302] The "understanding of relationship" has to do with empathy for another person, an ability to comprehend how that person is thinking and feeling about spiritual matters, which is at the heart of compassion. This understanding definitely precludes trying to get an A in evangelism or bragging about conversion or spiritual accomplishment, but honestly turning our thoughts from ourself to the other.

The appeal of this type of evangelism is noted by Anne Lamott: "Most of the people I know who have what I want—which is to say, purpose, heart, balance, gratitude, joy—are people with a deep sense of spirituality. They are people in community, who pray, or practice their faith; they are Buddhists, Jews, Christians—people banding together to work on themselves and for human rights. They follow a brighter light than the glimmer of their own candle; they are part of something beautiful." [Lamott, 100]

Lamott brings up a third and important aspect of community in her reference to working "for human rights." We may worship with a group of people, leave a generous offering for the support and "work" of the congregation, greet the other members politely after a service, exchange a few words, and forget about them all for another week. This is only a feeble start toward entering into community with a group. There is no substitute for spending time *doing* something with other people. The formation of bonds requires propinquity and many hours. This may mean peeling apples together with other members, participating in church fairs, attending discussion groups. It may also mean working in a special project of the congregation that clearly and directly helps people who need that help.

A significant danger arises here because, although we may all wish to help improve the lot of other people and promote peace among them, we often differ on the best way to do this. And very often differ strongly, based on who we are, how we think, and what we have experienced. This difference is the basis of political parties. As Norris remarks, "We are not individuals who have come together because we are like-minded. That is not a church, but a political party." [Norris, 272] As I noted earlier in discussing the need to combine intelligence with compassion, a congregation that advocates and acts on the means to an end, rather than supporting the value of the end, is courting problems. Some ministers preach sermons perhaps unconsciously in support of the positions of one political party or another, depending on how they are convinced that people may best express their love. Such ministers have strayed from the crucial and more challenging task of inspiring us to worship and take joy in the Eternal Spirit, and then in thanksgiving to love and act in love toward our family, neighbors, everyone we meet, and eventually the larger community. So inspired, we can then pursue the means of helping the larger community in the way we personally think will be most effective. There is no easier way to turn off people from a congregation than sermons and prayers that neglect the spiritual needs of a congregation in well-meaning but not well-thought-out efforts to promote political action.

Let us return to my original question: Can we be religious in the sense of living a fulfilling spiritual life without participating in group worship? I would answer that yes, we can, but our chances of so doing are greatly improved by joining a church community for group worship and taking advantage of its triple offerings: A long-considered body of thought about God's relationship to man, an established although perhaps developing way of "opening the heart to the reality of the sacred all around us," and the opportunity to participate in a caring community.

Can all the offerings touted above be found elsewhere? Yes, but not all at the same place. We can read theological books and articles and participate in discussion groups about the meaning of life and God. We can attend worship services of our choice as a visitor, and perhaps even join a congregation, remaining on the fringes. And we can belong to and actively participate in a club or association whose members work for what we consider a worthy purpose. For many, this combination is possible and effective.

We each have to search our hearts, find out who we are, and accept what we discover. It may be that for some of us full participation in a church community is not the way we can go, even when we wish it were.

◆   ◆   ◆

Those of us who choose to attend worship services of any religious group are going to run into writings that are considered revelations from God and stories that could not possibly be factually true. So let us take a look at these revelations and myths to see what they can hold for us.

DISCUSSION QUESTIONS

What kind of worship service feels most natural to you and puts you in a receptive mood? Do you respond to ritual, or do you prefer a very plain service?

What elements of a worship service, if any, throw you off?

Do certain doctrines of various churches puzzle or repel you? Which ones, and why? Can you understand how they developed?

What sacrament, if any, is meaningful to you, and in what way?

How do you feel about participating in a church community? Do you prefer the communal experience of working together to that of worshiping together, or the reverse?

12

REVELATION and MYTH

The images are outward, but their reflection is inward. [Campbell, 56-57]

How can we tell what is valid among the superstitions, fantasies, myths, stories, and multiple writings that purport to tell us about God and our relationship to him and his creation? Has God really "spoken" to certain individuals with particular messages at special times? And if so, how are we to distinguish God's voice from those of the individuals reporting what he has supposedly communicated? In fact, when he speaks to you and me, might it not instead be the voice of our own desires? And finally, of all this, what is really true and also relevant to us today?

Our personal doubts as to whether we are in fact hearing God speak to us lead to doubts concerning the testimony of others. And yet there are times, perhaps few and far between, when we *know* that we have had an experience of the Mystery, that we have been in direct communication with something above, below, and inside all of life. Such experiences of course are called epiphanies, which I have discussed in an earlier chapter. As to less vivid communications with God, we are often less sure, knowing that our ego and our desires can distort the messages from our conscience and our subconscious.

Jane Goodall and Nora Gallagher, the one an English anthropologist and environmentalist and the other an American reporter, both try to explain what they mean when they say that God has spoken to them. Goodall begins defensively: "Is it arrogant, presumptuous, to think that I might have heard the Voice of God? Not at all. We all do—that "still, small voice" that we speak of, telling us what we ought to do. That, I think, is the Voice of God. Of course, it is usually called the voice of conscience, and if we feel more comfortable with that definition, that's fine." [Goodall, 267] Gallagher's words show her difficulty in putting her thought into words: "That is how it is when I hear God speaking, when I see what could be or even what is, but too dimly to make it out. I can almost hear, I can almost see. I can almost touch the peace proclaimed. Sometimes I think that faith is only about increasing peripheral vision, peripheral hearing." [N. Gallagher, 59-60]

Gallagher's words bring to mind the "hearing back" common to all of us, when we have been paying no attention to someone speaking to us and then he pulls us up, accusing us of not hearing him. We then are able to "hear back" what he has said and triumphantly come up with his exact words. I suspect that something similar may have occurred when a person reports that God has spoken to him. Words have come up into his mind from his subconscious so that he has in fact sort of "heard" them, without benefit of sound waves.

Most of us rarely speak or write about God's communication with us, partially because we feel it is extremely intimate, also because we suspect that our listener would have doubts about our attributing our "revelation" to God, and finally because we find it difficult to put our experience into words without either blurring or trivializing it. And here we are back to the problem of language. One of the most common adjectives used to describe epiphanies is "ineffable," which means incapable of being expressed. And yet some epiphanies known by some people produce a strong urge to tell, in fact a demand to do so, that is part of the experience.

Such epiphanies are known by what are often referred to as "Spirit persons," who then speak out or put their revelations in written form. Spirit persons may be anyone, but in our day and age they tend to be ministers, rabbis, gurus, authors, sages, and prophets of all kinds. They have had strong spiritual experiences that cannot *not* be told, and they tell them in whatever language seems to them most fitting. So it has been throughout the ages. Jesus and the Buddha were obviously very powerful Spirit persons who dedicated their lives to telling others what they had received from God, the Mystery, the Ground of Being, whatever.

Each of these Spirit persons told and continues to tell it in his or her own way, in the language most meaningful to the individual and thought most likely to communicate at a particular time and within a particular culture. Most often, the language chosen consists of images. After all, what does the most accurate descriptive word for an epiphany—"ineffable"—communicate to anyone else? If you are going to say that you can't describe it, you might as well not even try!

One of the most accepted images is that of speech. Spirit persons say that God "said" this or that to them, because the images have to belong to human communication. I think that most of us have learned not to take literally the image of speaking, knowing that most of what we feel God has communicated to us has not been received in the form of sound waves (although certainly some people seem to have experienced God's messages in this way). We must learn to interpret intelligently many more images if we are to be able to understand what Spirit persons are trying to tell us.

In our culture especially, such interpretation has become difficult for the person not exposed early in life to the difference between fact and truth. Marcus Borg points out that "we live in the only culture in human history that has equated truth with factuality." [Borg, in an essay in *The Christian Century*, quoted by Norris, 190] The explanation probably has to do with our delight and pride in the exponential increase in our scientific discoveries over the past century. Somehow we have lost our understanding of the difference between what happens and its meaning.

Odd, is it not, because the concept is not that difficult to grasp. Norris tells of a five-year-old child who had no trouble with the concept, simply saying that "a myth is a story that isn't true on the outside, only on the inside." [Quoted by Norris, 120, from "Here All Dwell Free" by Gertrud Mueller Nelson]. Children learn this early in life even when they are too young to read stories by themselves. They know at the same time both that the stories their parents read to them didn't "*really* happen" and also that the moral they often carry is true. For example, in "The Little Engine That Could," children know that the story is not of a factual happening, that there never was nor ever will be a train that talks; and simultaneously they understand that the story tells something that is true, namely, that if you really believe you can do something and try very hard, often you can do it.

General difficulty with distinguishing between fact and truth in the Bible did not occur until the intelligentsia in western countries became preoccupied with and enamored of scientific fact toward the end of the nineteenth century. Gradually the ability to perceive the truth carried by nonfactual stories was lost. For example, biblical scholars began to find the differences between the stories in the three Gospels disconcerting and proceeded to throw out the baby with the bath water. Certainly readers of the Bible in the Middle Ages and earlier could not but know that the stories were told in different ways, but this knowledge did not make them say, "Oh, the authors of the Gospels have their facts wrong, so let us discard the Gospels as lies." They understood that the Gospels, even though what they said could perhaps not be relied upon as literal fact, as history, were telling something important, something that they felt transmitted the word of God and that they found relevant to their lives.

And so what is termed "higher criticism" of the Bible began, leading to the split that we see today. On the one side are people who, having had an immature or nonexistent religious faith, *did* throw out the baby with the bath water. William James, way back in the beginning of the twentieth century, had pointed out how illogical this was: "It does not follow, because our ancestors made so many errors of fact and mixed them with their religion, that we should therefore leave off being religious at all." [James, 388] Still others hung onto both the baby and the bath water. In reaction to the perceived challenge to Christianity, so-called true believers have loyally but irrationally been forming ranks and insisting that every word of the Bible is true, regardless of contradictions and obvious factual faults. One result is "creationism," which irrationally discards the facts discovered about the evolution of the earth, mankind, and other species.

Fortunately, there were those who carefully held the baby back while emptying the bath water. Not all scholars and theologians have taken a stand at one extreme or the other. Many have been delving carefully and deeply into the Bible, in particular the Gospels, to discover what the facts were, as in, exactly what did Jesus say? What do new discoveries of additional writings from that time reveal about what actually happened, about what words Jesus did in fact speak? One group, The Jesus Seminar, has actually been voting on how likely each saying is to have been uttered by Jesus himself. I find that interesting and helpful, but not vitally important. I am not waiting with bated breath to discover their conclusions, because how will that affect my spiritual life? Those I have been quoting often in this book—Marcus Borg, Bishop Spong, Thomas Hart, C. S. Lewis, William James—are among the writers who have chosen a rational path, viewing the Bible with the same critical historical eye that they would use on any other work of a different century. And while doing this, they have not closed the other eye, the spiritual eye, so to speak, that looks for meaning. I will quote here Bishop Spong, the self-named "believer in exile," to show that even those to the liberal side of center have no problem interpreting the Bible intelligently and spiritually at the same time:

> The point must be heard: the Gospels are first-century narrations based on first-century interpretations. Therefore they are a first-century filtering of the experience of Jesus. They have never been other than that. We must read them today not to discover the literal truth about Jesus, but rather to be led into the Jesus experience they were seeking to convey.... They are rather beautiful portraits painted by first-century Jewish artists, designed to point the reader

toward that which is in fact holy, accurate, and real. [Spong, 107-08]

Borg suggests a spiritual as well as intelligent approach to the Bible, writing that Scripture "is not to be treated as an object of belief but is to be lived within. It becomes a lens through which we 'see' God, life, and ourselves and a means by which our imaginations are shaped by the sacred." [Borg, *God*, 117]

The fear of losing religious beliefs because of scientific discoveries that seem to invalidate parts of the Bible is only one cause of the current retreat from middle-of-the-road Christianity. Another is the encrustation that has occurred in the form of superstitions and childish embroideries on the Christian message. Examples are the special holiness of objects that Jesus or some saint just might have touched and even pictures of Jesus as a sweet-faced and rather vapid young man of Aryan descent. Annie Dillard broadens the problem of superstition to include all religions, lamenting that the "presenting face of any religion is its mass of popular superstitions. It seems to take all the keenest thinkers of every religion in every generation to fend off this clamoring pack." [Dillard, 78]

Still another deterrent to understanding the Bible as the word of God, literal or not literal, is the portrait drawn of him primarily but not exclusively in the Old Testament, as a vengeful power who favored the Israelites over all other peoples and who derided mankind for its foolishness. There is no way that this god can be reconciled with the God of love preached by Jesus. It is not just a matter of power or of the incomprehensible (to us) disaster and evil in the world. It is the prejudice and vengefulness of the deity as seen many times in what he says and does in parts of the Bible. However, the inconsistencies with the loving and just deity of Jesus disappear as soon as the text is examined and understood as the work of specific people at a particular time in history whose own needs and failings were reflected in their idea of their god.

So far, I have been considering primarily Christianity, because in one form or another it has been the religion of the majority in America. Revelation is not limited to one religion, of course. People have been interacting with the Mystery as long as there have been people and no doubt will do so as long as our species survives. Revelation is far from a one-time, one-religion, or one-sect occurrence. God has been revealing himself—or, put the other way, people have been discovering him—throughout the ages, each in their own unique way, depending upon the individual and the culture. The more spiritually perceptive in any culture have been describing the Mystery in more spiritual terms than the less perceptive, who may have simply known him as the force of nature. As cultures became more sophisticated, the spiritual content changed accordingly.

We are now in an age that seems to yearn, not for religion, but for spiritual experience. The nature of what we perceive, of our revelations, is changing. While our scholars and theologians are not differing substantially in their message from what has been perceived for aeons as the heart of Christianity, their emphasis is different. It is more on God as the Spirit and Mystery within our daily life, with careful disparagement of the image of a God "up there." Not surprisingly, since I am a part of the present culture, this is also my song. As long as people are tuned to the spiritual basis of their lives, they will be discovering God in ways unique to themselves. And so will we in our daily lives, although only a few of us may feel called to put what we perceive into words. Bishop Spong looks to the future with hope for new growth. He sees "life as existing somewhere on the being-becoming spectre.... That would not be unlike a prepubescent twelve year old thinking that he or she has experienced all that life has to offer, only to live into the postpubescent experiences that no twelve year old could possibly contemplate." [Spong, 214]

Not only is there a future for revelation, there is also a past, going way back before Jesus, before the Buddha, before written history. I refer of course to myth. Joseph Campbell is the modern guru of myth, and thanks to him and interviewer Bill Moyers, the television series on the subject has spread the word to a great many people. Not that Campbell is the sole supporter of the value of myths. Not by a long shot. For example, here is Borg, writing succinctly as always, on the subject: "In short, a myth is a story about God and us. As such, myths can be both true and powerful, even though they are symbolic narratives and not straightforward historical reports. Though not literally true, they can be really true; though not factually true, they can be actually true." [Borg, *God*, 101]

Even in Joseph Campbell's writing, I have found no clearer definition of a myth than that given by the five-year-old child and quoted above—a story that isn't true on the outside, only on the inside. We should add that the word "myth" is usually used to refer to a story of a culture that has been passed on for so many years that the storyteller has long been forgotten. The story has become a public, group story.

Campbell explains what myths do for humankind, why we tell these stories. I will let him speak for himself. First, they "bring us into a level of consciousness that is spiritual" [Campbell, 14] because they are "clues to the spiritual potentialities of the human life." [Campbell, 5] So far, so good, because finding the spiritual level is step one. Their subject matter has to do "with the themes that have supported human life, built civilizations, and informed religions over the millennia…with deep inner problems, inner mysteries, inner thresholds of passage, and if you don't know what the guide-signs are along the way, you have to work it out yourself. [Campbell, 4] We go to myths for "an experience of being alive, so that our life experiences on the purely physical plane will have resonances within our own innermost being and reality, so that we actually feel the rapture of being alive. That's what it's all finally about, and that's what these clues help us to find within ourselves." [Campbell, 5] Or again, "To see life as a poem and yourself participating in a poem is what the myth does for you." [Campbell, 55]

Myths also have more complex functions. They tell us that "at the bottom of the abyss comes the voice of salvation...At the darkest moment comes the light." [Campbell, 39] They also help us "to be in accord with the grand symphony that this world is, to put the harmony of our own body in accord with that harmony." [Campbell, 55] A more complex task that they attempt is to reconcile "the mind to this brutal precondition of all life, which lives by the killing and eating of life." [Campbell, 55] Succinctly, they bring hope, harmony, and a recognition of what we feel as the cruelty of the creator.

Myths are told and retold in all cultures. Campbell has found the "same stories in American Indian lore, Hinduism, Arthurian medieval, religion. The themes are timeless, and the inflection is to the culture." [Campbell, 11] He explains that since "the inspiration comes from the unconscious, and since the unconscious minds of the people of any single small society have much in common, what the shaman or seer brings forth is something that is waiting to be brought forth in everyone." [Campbell, 58] He gives us a useful image, writing that it's "as though the same play were taken from one place to another, and at each place the local players put on local costumes and enact the same old play." [Campbell, 39]

Following the same line of thought a bit further, he compares myths with dreams, because they both arise from the subconscious: "A dream is a personal experience of that deep, dark ground that is the support of our conscious lives, and a myth is the society's dream. The myth is the public dream and the dream is the private myth." [Campbell, 40]

Many religious ceremonies originate in myths and from them derive their power. As Campbell puts it, mythology "has a great deal to do with the stages of life, the initiation ceremonies as you move from childhood to adult responsibilities, from the unmarried state into the married state. All of those rituals are mythological rites." [Campbell, 11] These ceremonies also have to do with change of season, and so "all through the year keep you in mind of the eternal core of all that changes in time." [Campbell, 10]

So how do myths matter to us as we consider God's communication with us? I think they tell us to "lighten up" about what actually did and didn't happen. The very fact that stories such as Noah and the flood and the coming of the Wise Men have been told for years and years verifies their inner content as of value to us. Rather than considering the recurrence of a particular story in one civilization after another as proof that a story is not factual but a product of one person's or one civilization's imagination, we should take those similarities between stories as verification of their message-carrying capability. Why should we all tell the same story, year after year, age after age, aeon after aeon, if it is meaningless? Perhaps, really *indeed*, we should listen more carefully and find what a particular story may tell us.

Christmas comes, and with it the story of the Virgin Mary traveling to Bethlehem to give birth to the Christ Child and laying him in a manger in a stable, because there was no room at the inn. We should resist our secular society's urge to say, "But I doubt very strongly that the story is factual. A *virgin* giving birth? Come on, now. And we have no historical verification that Jesus was born in Bethlehem. All this is just a pretty story!" Yes, it is a pretty story, in fact a beautiful and a powerful story. A story that has been meaningful to people throughout the world for close to two thousand years. Perhaps we should pretend for the moment, pretend throughout a Christmas Eve service perhaps, that everything in the New Testament story read to the congregation is really true. (Tomorrow we can note the differences between the Gospel stories of the birth, as a starter, and come back to sensible reality!) If we let ourselves float with the story, if we follow it imaginatively, we just may come out of the church feeling that God cherishes the poor, humble, and uneducated of this world, that he does enter history and even our own lives, that he may be trusted, and above all that there is hope, for the world and for us. We may even become aware that the angels *do* sing for joy. Less skeptical, perhaps more intuitive, and certainly more spiritual persons have received these blessings on Christmas Eve. Surely we might humbly put out our own hand for a blessing.

God, the Spirit, the Mystery, the Ground of our Being has been revealing himself to people from the beginning of time; he continues to do so, to us and to our neighbor; and he has promised that he will do so until the end of time. It is up to us to let our hearts and spirits hear.

◆　　◆　　◆

One topic that recurs in myths and revelations concerns what happens to us after we die. The idea of an afterlife of some sort occurs in almost every culture. In ours, this afterlife is usually referred to in most simplistic terms as heaven for those who have been good and hell for those who have been bad. The next chapter focuses on the difficult and murky subject of the afterlife and heaven.

DISCUSSION QUESTIONS

What criteria do you use to distinguish between the "voice of God" and your own desires?

What criteria do you use to judge whether what others claim is the "voice of God" really is so?

Have you been bothered by either the inconsistencies or the factual inaccuracies in the Gospels and other parts of the Bible? If so, have they affected either your thinking about religion or your spiritual life?

Has the apparent vengefulness and prejudice of the God of the Old Testament puzzled or disturbed you? Does the cultural and historical explanation of this satisfy you? In what way, if any, is the Old Testament still relevant to us today in our discovery of God's nature?

What myths appeal to you from among the many outside the Christian faith? Do you agree with Joseph Campbell that "at each place the local players put on local costumes and enact the same old play"?

Have you been able to enjoy the Christmas stories without questioning their factual accuracy?

13

HEAVEN and THE AFTERLIFE

Joy is the serious business of Heaven. [Lewis, *Prayer*, 93]

Heaven is one of those words that easily produce a smirk on the face of someone who thinks he has "moved beyond" the Christian religion, or more accurately, beyond his immature conception of what that religion—or in fact any religion—is all about. He thinks that "heaven" means to Christians a pretty, carefree abode of disembodied souls, all dancing around an assembly of angels, with a bearded and white-robed God sitting contentedly in the center of all the merrymakers. Probably taking place up in the sky somewhere as well.

Heaven in the Christian religion is the term for an idea that has sprung from spiritual experiences and intuitions widely shared by mankind. The idea is basically that a perfect existence—complete happiness—is possible for us, somewhere, sometime, somehow. What an odd notion, really. When you consider the world as we know it, with its unhappiness, tragedies, natural disasters, evil, and all sorts of misery, why would anyone think that all that could disappear and that such a thing as a perfect existence come into being? Even people who have lived as selflessly as possible—an approach that should according to our philosophers and theologians lead to happiness—have not found a perfect existence here on earth. So perhaps after death? Here is the connection between heaven and the after-life. We feel that heaven is possible, and if not here during our lifetimes, then perhaps after death.

The possibility of heaven (or paradise) is reflected perhaps most clearly in the idea expressed in the Garden of Eden of the Old Testament, where male and female are described as walking with God in perfect contentment. Similar myths appear in other cultures, all trying to tell us that complete happiness is possible. John Milton took up the story in his *Paradise Lost*. In poetry, there is William Wordsworth's *Intimations of Immortality*, directly to the point as he writes of newborn babes as "trailing clouds of glory as [they] come," and that "Heaven lies about us in our infancy." His poem expresses our sense that heaven is somehow implanted in our memory and so becomes an aspiration for us. Despite all evidence to the contrary, in our insides most of us seem to have the image of a perfect life as attainable and yet never attained.

Wendell Berry writes that heaven "floats among us like a cloud and is the realest thing we know and the last to be captured, the least to be possessed by anybody for himself. It is like a grain of mustard seed, which you cannot see among the crumbs of the earth where it lies. It is like the reflection of the trees on the water." [Berry, *Crow*, 351]

The idea that complete happiness—heaven—is possible has been expressed by prophets, sages, poets, and priests. They perceive heaven as known to us in fits and starts during our lifetime and perhaps in some way after death. It is the spiritual state to which we aspire here and now, and which we know somewhat in brief epiphanies but which we can never quite reach or hold onto. Religious skeptic Bishop Spong writes that for him heaven is a partial experience during life that provides the hope for a complete experience after death: "When my being is enhanced by love, called to a new reality by love, introduced through love to limitless freedom, then I believe that I have touched that which is timeless, eternal, and real. My confidence in eternal life, life beyond the limits of finitude and earth, is found in that experience." [Spong, 218] Again: "I stand here convinced that there is something real beyond my ultimate limits. I have but tasted it. So I embrace this vision and live in this hope." [Spong, 218]

Bishop Spong, like most contemporary theologians, spends few pages on the concept of an afterlife and certainly attempts no descriptions. However, several notions about heaven as a destination after death, even in our sophisticated age, have still not disappeared. Now, far be it from me to say that the various pictures people have of the afterlife are not in some sense true. Certainly what happens after death cannot be known by any of us and, to my way of thinking, that is just as well. We certainly have no "need to know," much as we would like to. Since it is obvious that we cannot find the answer to our questions concerning what if anything happens after death, it is rather remarkable that so much time has been spent both in trying to do so and even in trying to prove that there is no such a thing as an afterlife.

One notion of heaven after death is that we will recognize each other after we die and, if we have been good, "go to Heaven," where we will pick up our old relationships.

The complications that might arise from such a situation are the basis for jokes of all sorts. Nevertheless, the notion has not completely disappeared. I was surprised a few months ago to see it surface with a casual acquaintance. In the course of my volunteer work, I have been visiting a woman of little education but much common sense and charm, whose son died six years ago, at the age of seventy. She and her son's second wife, whom I shall call Grace, still correspond weekly. I met Grace briefly and have learned more about her because many of her letters have been read aloud to me. She is kind, pleasant, and as far as I can judge, not in any way unusual or foolish. She is not a member of any church. When the son's first wife died earlier this year of complications from Alzheimer's disease, Grace reacted with distress, although she never had met her, because she feared that her deceased husband would "get together" with his just-deceased first wife. In other words, she was jealous! I must report that the elderly lady I visit was gently amused, as was I. I was also taken aback to see such an idea still alive in our secular times. She apparently thought of the afterlife as a distinct place. It was as if the deceased husband had entered a different room and now his first wife, on dying, was able to go in with him while Grace, still alive, was kept out. I should add that she said nothing, however, about wanting to die herself so that she could interrupt the couple's possible intimacy!

For several reasons, I do not want to smirk about the idea that we recognize each other after death and take up our old relationships. The first, of course, is that we cannot know that something is *not* true. The second is that we know nothing whatever about what happens after we die, so saying yes or no concerning any idea on the subject is foolishness. The third reason is more significant, and it derives from a memorial service that I attended about five years ago at a large urban church. (Coincidentally in this context, the service was for my first husband.)

The aging minister, who had been the senior minister in this congregation during his prime, was highly respected. He had no doubt preached at many a funeral and held the hand of many a grieving mate. He himself had lost his first wife some thirty years ago, had remarried, and subsequently had raised a second family. In other words, he had been there. He knew much, much more than I about death and grieving. The point here is that his sermon, and indeed the entire service, was based on the consoling idea that we would meet our beloved again in heaven. He kept coming back to this idea.

I was a bit puzzled, since this minister was anything but unsophisticated, and so I did not dismiss it out of hand. Instead, I tried to incorporate his idea into my own thinking to see if it might fit or perhaps cause me to rearrange some of my thinking. What I came up with was this: first, of course, that no one could know; and second, that the fact that we will never again see the deceased is the cut that hurts most, particularly at first—the "never" is so unpalatable; and the second led into the third, which is that since seeing the deceased again is wanted so desperately, it is an important element in what heaven would be for the living mate, who feels that there could be no heaven, no complete happiness, without the deceased mate. So maybe in some sense it is true. I know that the minister believed it as well as preached it. And it just might be that he knew a bit more about the subject than I. At least I was reminded that one should not dismiss other' convictions out of hand as naïve.

Another common notion is that we gain entrance to heaven after death by being good here on earth. It relegates heaven completely to the afterlife. Heaven is for the good, and hell is for the bad. The idea has an attractive simplicity, but it does not correspond at all with life as we know it. Most of us have had moments of heaven and moments of hell. I have known well several people who were clearing living in what could be termed hell for them. I still shudder at remembering their continuing psychological/spiritual agony. Watts writes that "Hell consists not in being deprived of union, but in willful failure to appreciate it." [Watts, 80] C. S. Lewis talks of understanding hell "in its aspect of privation. All your life an unattainable ecstasy has hovered just beyond the grasp of your consciousness. The day is coming when you will wake to find, beyond all hope, that you have attained it, or else, that it was within your reach and you have lost it forever." [Lewis, *Pain*, 148]

Wendell Berry writes on the relationship of goodness to a possible afterlife with a poet's inspired wisdom and imagination. This quotation is a long one, but well worth careful reading:

> I imagine the dead waking, dazed, into a shadowless light in which they know themselves altogether for the first time. It is a light that is merciless until they can accept its mercy; by it they are at once condemned and redeemed. It is Hell until it is Heaven. Seeing themselves in that light, if they are willing, they see how far they have failed the only justice of loving one another; it punishes them by their own judgment. And yet, in suffering that light's awful clarity, in seeing themselves within it, they see its forgiveness and its beauty, and are consoled. In it they are loved completely, even as they have been, and so are changed into what they could not have been but what, if they could have imagined it, they would have wished to be. [Berry, *World*, 150-51]

So what do our spiritual guides say about heaven as a possible after-life experience and a reward for the righteous? Contemporary Christian skeptic Bishop Spong, whose sense of an afterlife for mankind derives from his experience of loving, writes: "I do assert that one prepares for eternity not by being religious and keeping the rules, but by living fully, loving wastefully, and daring to be all that each of us has the capacity to be." [Spong, 218-19] Another approach also emphasizing the here-and-now-ness of heaven is taken by Scott Russell Sanders, author and university teacher of literature and writing. Speaking of his sixtyish high school science teacher, whose passion and pleasure in the natural world were so great that they in fact invited the ridicule of her students, he wrote: "She taught me that the genius is not in our look-ing but in what we see. If only we could be adequate to the given world, we need not dream of paradise." [Sanders, 186] Heaven is here for those who can see. Perhaps it is not exactly the heaven we envision or would devise, but it is heaven nonetheless for those who can per-ceive it, and possibly the only heaven there is or will be.

While many of us recognize that the concept of heaven is relevant to our earthly lives, that we may know a bit of it now, and that it is what we aspire to while still living, we cannot easily get rid of the basic desire to know what happens to us and our loved ones after we die. The idea of becoming nothing is hard to imagine and not to be swallowed with-out great effort. And we somehow feel that death is robbing us of our most precious possession, namely life. We forget that we never earned nor indeed owned our life. Sanders points out that we "can lose our life only because it has been given to us." [Sanders, 163]

Some of us bravely say that we live on in our children and their chil-dren, in their bodies, their souls, and certainly their memories. As to the last, perhaps for a few years. We may tell ourselves that our love for others during our lifetime lives on, because love never dies. Such thoughts provide little consolation. And so we try to leave something more specific to them, something very much of ourselves to them, per-haps some work of our hands or minds—a quilt that we have stitched, a business that we have established, a book that we have written. We cling to this earth and do not want all of ourselves to have left it when we die. Our great difficulty in accepting the fact of death is reflected not only in our efforts to imagine an after-life but also in the denials—that many people are strangely quick to express—that there is an afterlife. Some of us make brave attempts to face the possibility that when we die, that is it, the end. The traditional Christian persists in hope. Hart writes that what we need "is a reason to hope. The death and resurrection of Jesus gives us that reason, revealing to us that with God death is never the last word. Life is." [Hart, 131]

My personal thoughts on the subject have to do with time and its relationship to the idea of eternity. Watts says that eternity "is not unending time; it is an indestructible present." [Watts, 85] The present and eternity are somehow one, with time being the way that we mortals are able to perceive life. Echoes of the Eternal Now concept. C. S. Lewis writes that "our creaturely limitation is that our fundamentally timeless reality can be experienced by us only in the mode of succession." [Lewis, *Prayer,* 110] Turning to the afterlife based on this same concept, he imagines a situation wherein the "dead might experience a time which was not quite so linear as ours—it might, so to speak, have thickness as well as length. Already in this life we get some thickness whenever we learn to attend to more than one thing at once. One can suppose this increased to any extent so that though, for them as for us, the present is always becoming the past, yet each present contains unimaginably more than ours." [Lewis, *Prayer,* 109-10]

Another ancient and widespread notion, based on the assumption that we retain our human limitations after death, is that our death, as did our birth, leads into another reality that may or may not involve time. (Reincarnation assumes that death leads into the same reality, although at a later point.) Birth is the beginning, and death is both an end and also a beginning leading to another end, which is also a beginning. And so on. Like birth, death is usually a difficult and painful experience for at least a short period of time. And perhaps is similarly forgotten. This possibility has great intellectual and emotional appeal to me.

However, in our wiser moments, in times of spiritual light, many of us realize that we really do not need to know anything about the afterlife. If we have faith in God's compassion and power, we can leave it to him. Remember Jesus's comments on the afterlife: "In my Father's house are many mansions." Loosely translated but I think accurately interpreted, that means, "Don't worry about it. God will take care of you." Jesus probably also meant that knowing exactly what would happen after death is not necessary, and, perhaps, that he himself didn't know or in fact concern himself about the afterlife. He saw it as in God's hands.

The more faith we have in God's power and love, the less we will worry about death and the possibility of an afterlife. We will trust him to take care of all that. And the more we perceive God as the Mystery, the Spirit, the Ground of Our Being within our daily lives, the less we will think in terms of heaven and hell as reward and punishment after death. What matters is the now.

◆   ◆   ◆

And what are two important elements of the "now," often neglected by thinkers of all persuasions? Laughter and work. So let us turn from the heavy stuff and consider these special gifts to humankind.

DISCUSSION QUESTIONS

How much of your grieving at someone's death is about what will happen to the person who has died and how much is about the emptiness of your own life without that person?

Does the concept of heaven in any way lessen your sorrow or lighten your grieving?

Do you believe that your actions in this life will determine your afterlife, if any? In what way?

Does the concept of the resurrection of Jesus, whether in spiritual or bodily form, affect your thoughts about the afterlife?

Do you find the idea of eternity as "indestructible present" intriguing and relevant to daily living or confusing and esoteric?

Do you prefer the idea of reincarnation back into this world to the idea of being born into another world, or the reverse?

14

LAUGHTER and WORK

Laugh, and the world laughs with you;
Weep, and you weep alone.
[Ella Wheeler Wilcox, "Solitude"]

Why laughter and work together in one chapter? Very simply, because I perceive them as two especially wonderful gifts of God for which we rarely give him sufficient thanks. And both are of great value every day. What would life be like without laughter with our friends and enough work to do so that we know ourselves useful? In brief, they matter. If they disappear from your daily life, and sometimes they do, then you really learn their worth.

Do you remember that shortest sentence in the Bible, "Jesus wept."? [John 11:35] I have often wished there were a parallel sentence, "Jesus laughed." Surely, Jesus must have laughed many times. He was an apparently healthy young man in the company of other young men; he must sometimes have been merry with them. We know that he attended a wedding ceremony and turned water into wine, but there is no indication that he was being anything more than cooperative with his mother and his host. Recently, I saw a postcard-size picture of Jesus affixed to the wall at a friend's home. I glanced and glanced again—and couldn't believe what I was seeing. There was a picture of Jesus with a smile, really a grin, on his face. Inside me, I said, "Yes! The sun must have shown *sometime* during Jesus's life."

The sky is overcast in the Gospels, almost always, and in fact throughout most of the Old and New Testaments. I checked my concordance for words translated as "laugh" and "laughter," and it revealed eight "laughs" and two "laughters" in the Old Testament, and only two of the first and one of the second in the New. Before you start to think that the Old Testament prophets and seers were a more frolicking group than the early Christians, let me tell you that the laughter, with one exception, was the laughter of derision. The exception was in Psalm 126:1-2, "When the Lord restored the fortunes of Zion, we were like those who dream. Then our mouth was filled with laughter, and our tongue with shouts of joy." Two of the three New Testament references are grim, however. In Luke 6:25, Jesus in the Sermon on the Mount says, and "Woe to you that laugh now, for you shall mourn and weep," while James 4:9 predicts much the same thing: "Let your laughter be turned to mourning and your joy to dejection." Fortunately, we find one positive use of the word "laugh," also in the Sermon on the Mount: "Blessed are you that weep now, for you shall laugh." [Luke 6:21] We at least know that Jesus was acquainted with laughter and thought it a sign of joy, even though it was never recorded that he himself laughed. Words translated as "joy" and "joyful," however, are plentiful in both the Old and New Testaments, usually in terms of promise.

There are many kinds of laughter and many different situations that give rise to each. These have been well and fully described by Robert Provine, a behavioral neuroscientist, in his recent book *Laughter: A Scientific Investigation*, which cannot be ignored by anyone writing about laughter today. He calls laughter a "harlequin that shows two faces—one smiling and friendly, the other dark and ominous," [Provine, 2] like the derisive laughter referred to in the Old Testament.

Provine's study is based on biological fact and empirical data. He recorded and analyzed with sound spectrographs twelve hundred "laugh episodes," which consist of the comment just before the laughter and all laughter occurring within one second after the first "onset." He contrasts this approach with what he terms the "prescientific literature on laughter, comedy, and humor," by such notables as Plato, Aristotle, Descartes, Hobbes, Kant, Schopenhauer, Darwin, Freud, and

Bergson. He points out that laughter by itself, not combined with humor, has received little attention.

Laughter is a fascinating book with all sorts of interesting information, only some of which is relevant here. Provine says flatly that "laughter is about relationships," pointing out that his analysis revealed that "most laughter did not follow anything resembling a joke, storytelling, or other formal attempt at humor." [Provine, 40] On the spectrograph, laughter is like "a series of evenly spaced sonic beads on a string." [Provine, 57] He devotes a chapter to the laughter of the higher apes, who make a "breathy, pantlike sound," because, unlike humans, they vocalize during both inhalation and exhalation, whereas our laughter is only during exhalation. The laughter occurs during rough play and tickling, mainly with the young. Human laughter he calls "an ancient signal, a sound more like an animal call or cry than human speech." [Provine, 55] When you think about it, that is true! He further notes that the "vowellike 'ha-ha-ha's' that parse the outward breath in modern human laughter is [sic] one step removed from the archetypal huffing and puffing that signaled laughter and play in our ancient ancestors." [Provine, 97] For human beings, it is an "unconscious response to social and linguistic cues." [Provine, 2]

Many of Provine's scientifically based conclusions verify what most of us already know about laughter. Laughter is something that is shared. It is heartier and lasts longer if the laughers look into each other's eyes. The more people, the more laughter. Rarely do we laugh when alone, and even then it may in a sense be shared with the author of a book or article whose words have given rise to the laughter or with the studio audience (or laugh track) of a television comedy. Provine's research also showed that speakers laugh more than their audiences, females more often than males, and less dominant persons more often than dominant.

The contagion of laughter is well known—leading to laugh tracks for the media and laugh boxes like the Tickle-Me Elmo toy popular recently. Similarly, the euphoria that results from a good, hearty laugh is no secret. These two aspects of laughter have been used in large groups, both secular and religious. In the 1970's and 1980's, there were conferences of the International Society of Humor Studies and a spate of books on humor. Laughing Clubs International, formed in Bombay in 1995, now has over 100 branches meeting daily in public parks for the express purpose of stimulating laughter in each other in combination with exercises to promote it. Their general purpose is the health that laughter is supposed to engender. *Time* magazine reported in 1994 the growing number of "laughing revivals" of religious groups, similar to the more exuberant practices of some Pentecostal churches.

The laughter that I have in mind here, which is often taken for granted, is the hearty kind, shared by two people looking straight into each other's eyes. It is not derisive as in the Old Testament, nor is it a polite or nervous tittering. It provides a wonderful relief from whatever one needs relief from—tension, fear, overwork, loneliness, whatever—while at the same time saying to the other guy, "We are friends. I like you."

The beneficial effects of laughter didn't really get my attention until eight years ago when I started my "elderwork," which consists of weekly visits of an hour or two with each of eight elderly people who either are "shut-ins," cannot leave the house without help, or suffer from isolation and loneliness. I had been aware of Norman Cousins's book about laughter as a cure for illness, *Anatomy of an Illness*, but I had been fortunate enough not to have had to deal with a serious illness myself or in my immediate family, so I didn't think much about laughter. Or about what the lack of it might mean.

Being a cheerful person, I fell easily into the habit of kidding around with my elderly clients and laughing about all sorts of crazy little things. Soon I discovered that, even though I encountered an atmosphere of gloom and doom in the house when I entered, on my departure there were smiles (presumably not because I was at last departing). I asked myself if this was simply because I had really listened to them unburden their hearts and minds for an hour or two, or was it because someone, anyone, had been with them to relieve their loneliness. And then I began to notice that, as I left the house, more than a few of my clients would say something like, "Oh, didn't we have ourselves a good laugh today! I haven't laughed like that in a long time." At that point, I started to pay attention to the benefits of laughter and go out of my way to find at least one thing about which the client and I could share a hearty laugh during each visit. It would have helped if I were an effective joke teller, which I am not. But when I would occasionally attempt a joke that I couldn't resist and thought I just might be able to tell properly, we would usually find that I was so bad at it that we had to laugh not at the joke but at my failure to tell it well.

One day, driving away from a client's home after she had remarked on our laughter, I began to consider seriously what a blessing laughter can be. Here is this weird sound, nothing like words, coming up from the human throat, quite spontaneously and often uncontrollably. We inherit the sound from our ape ancestors, whose laughter is similar in sound and similarly caused. The apes laugh primarily in response to chase-and-tickle, as do our human children. Only as we grow and develop do the causes of laughter begin to include humor, an intellectual phenomenon. For both apes and humans, laughter is a sharing that begets friendship and joy. And it can come to anyone, spontaneously, contagiously, almost unavoidably, without thought or intent. What a gift from the creator of this immense and puzzling universe!

My elderwork also drew my attention to the psychological value of having work to do, because the lack of a useful and necessary occupation was clearly at least one identifiable cause of many of my clients' depression. (I use that term here to mean the ordinary depression most people have occasionally, not the clinical depression for which drug therapy is often prescribed.) When people are about to retire, they usually look forward to doing all the things they have postponed, pursuing a neglected hobby or sport, reading all the books laid aside for later, listening to all the recorded music they have acquired and had no time for, and traveling to fascinating places. The list of all they will do when they have the time is endless. And then, to their surprise, they some-how begin to lose their taste for all that pleasure. The motivation just isn't there. What may soon seem endless is time itself. Although books, articles, and pamphlets a-plenty warn future retirees that they need not only money but an occupation to make them happy, many people ignore the advice. This is okay for awhile. And then comes boredom. Have you ever noticed that retired persons, when asked how they like their retirement, always want to tell you right away how "busy" they are? This is the accepted way of either denying the problem of bore-dom and too much time or telling you that they are handling it alright.

I know, because I have been there myself. I retired to a Massachu-setts hill town with a new husband, two horses, and several dogs and cats. We got ourselves settled, and then I said, "What now? I don't want to ride horseback and walk dogs all day everyday, and I certainly don't want to make a second career of housekeeping!" Fortunately, I did have volunteering for *something* in the back of my head, and a newspaper article about elderwork started me on my present path. My volunteering came about partially because I did want to do something helpful for someone with my spare time, but also because I could feel a bit of panic starting up inside. I am an energetic, fast-moving person for whom the thought of nothing to do is very, very unsettling. So I launched myself into a second career of elderwork, treating it as if I were being paid to do it, meaning that only my own illness or really rotten weather would keep me "from my appointed rounds." In other words, getting up in the morning and not feeling like visiting one of my clients was no excuse. For me, I did the right thing. I had found my work.

As I am using the word, "work" comprises a broader band of activi-ties than a compensated job or a volunteer position. I have come to think that an activity becomes work and assumes its benefits when the person working considers it so. In other words, it is defined in the mind of the person doing it. Of course, during most of our lives, paid work—what everyone considers work—is necessary to earn a living.

We do it because we have to do it to acquire food, shelter, and clothing for ourselves and our family, and also to keep the family members clean, fed, and going about their business, be it a job or school. We work without realizing that we are blessed to have a required activity.

However, work that is excessive is not a blessing. It can be back-breaking if there is too much of it or if it is the wrong kind for us. Echoes of Genesis: "In the sweat of your face you shall eat bread." [Gen. 3:19] Labor in coal mines, in labor camps, or by children come to mind first, but we must not forget that in our society the stress of competitive white-collar jobs, often requiring too many hours to bring home the bacon of "success," may be equally injurious to the body and spirit.

As I observed my clients, all homebound, and so obviously no longer having a job or volunteer position, I perceived that a range of other activities could be and really were considered work for them and gave them the same benefits that younger people received from work. So I came to define it as an activity requiring effort that we *have* to do or *feel* we have to do, and often as not we think of it as something not particularly agreeable. Coming back to my personal example, I don't have to volunteer for the elderly, but I *feel* I have to and want to view it as my work. No one requires me to do it, and other people may not consider that I am in fact working.

Still other activities for which one receives no compensation and which seem not to be work to someone else may indeed be work to the persons doing them. For example, when a retired man with arthritis takes a long walk daily on the advice of a doctor, can he consider that work? I think so, because it is something he feels he *has* to do, it requires effort, and he may well not feel like doing it. When he goes ahead and takes that walk, it provides him with the psychological benefits that a job gives a younger person.

So what are the psychological benefits of work? They are numerous and varied, not only for the elderly but for those who are younger and even for children, whose familiar question, "What'll I do now?" still rings in my ears. If we have too little to do with our time—a situation for most of my elderly clients and some children—we are happy to find some work that will fill up our day, a benefit that the too-busy young adult and middle-aged person might not realize, but one not to be discounted. A second benefit accrues if our work helps someone in some way, because we feel useful and valuable to someone other than ourself, and our self-image grows. A third benefit has to do with community. For the elderly, work that helps others makes them feel that they are still within the active community, rather than relegated to the far edges among the "useless old." Many a time an elderly client, whose arthritic hands have finally made her give up even knitting or crocheting for her friends, has asked me, "But what *good* am I to anyone?" The young who are just joining the work force often feel proud not only because of work accomplished but also because they are at last becoming a part of the active adult community.

Even if the work benefits no one but ourselves, because we must expend effort and often do not really want to do the work, we gain self-respect when we make ourselves do it. This is a fourth benefit. Having finished, we experience a sense of accomplishment that increases our feeling of self-worth. Depending upon what work we are doing, we may also be keeping our body or our mind active and taking our thoughts from our worries and our aches and pains—number five. A final bonus is that, if we have work that we must do, our free time is that much more pleasurable. If all our time is available to play, play itself soon loses its value.

To really appreciate the benefits of work and make us thankful for it, let us glance in summary fashion at the harm that may result from a lack of work. It decreases or eliminates our self-respect, our sense of ourselves as part of a community, and any feeling of accomplishment. It devalues our recreation, it lets our minds and bodies fail from lack of use, and it gives us too much time with nothing to do but worry about ourselves and our problems.

I recently read a novel by Carol Shields that had as its major theme the value of work. Here is an explicit hymn to its value, expressing vividly all the points I have been making above. The author is talking about a fortyish man by the name of Larry, whose occupation is landscaping, specializing in maze design. He is in the throes of a mid-life crisis.

> ...He's worried sick at the moment about the distance that's grown between himself and his wife, about the night terrors that trouble his only child, about money, about broken or neglected friendships, about the pressure of too much silence, about whether his hedges will weather the winter, but he is, nevertheless, plugged into the planet. He's part of the action, part of the world's work, a cog in the great turning wheel of desire and intention.
>
> The day will arrive in his life when work—devotion to work, work's steady pressure and application—will be all that stands between himself and the bankruptcy of his soul.. "At least you have your work," his worried, kind-hearted friends will murmur, and if they don't, if they forget the availability of this single consolation—well then, he'll say it to himself: *at least I have my work.*
> [Shields, *Larry's Party*, 77]

I haven't mentioned any biblical references to the benefits of work and our need to be thankful for it—because I have found none. The primary reason is that leisure is a relatively new thing under the sun. Certainly in biblical times, constant work was necessary just to live, except perhaps for the very rich. Only recently have our practical scientific advances made possible long periods of time in which work just to survive is no longer required for many of us. How wonderful, we say, and then we think more deeply about it. Some of us regret having retired and find part-time jobs, or like me are delighted to retire and do something different with our lives. Still others jump quickly into all the leisure-time activities they can find, preferably with others the same age, and hope that the fun will last, which it rarely does. The less wise or less fortunate begin to feel useless, lonely for their friends still on the job, somewhat bored, and eventually depressed as their self-esteem sinks to a new low.

So what is the answer? I think it is the same one that is appropriate for the young. We need to try to discover what God is telling us to do. Rephrasing the answer, we need to search for our deepest wanting. And also look to our conscience, which will tell us to find a way to help others. This is the message of all religions, writ deep inside us. Then it is up to us to discover how to do these things, to fill in the specifics, to find the avenues and the people.

If anything is God-given, and at the same time a direct challenge requiring response, it is leisure, whether it comes early in life because riches make employment unnecessary or late in life because we have saved enough money to live comfortably without a full-time job. Leisure is the new challenge of our age for the many people who have been able to retire while they are still physically and mentally healthy. And if our life is indeed "generally oriented to God," as Hart phrased it, we will have the opportunity to both search for avenues for helping others and also respond to our deepest wanting. Thus we may fulfill and complete ourselves as unique human beings. By the time we reach our sixties, we should have made sufficient acquaintance with our heart and identified our abilities accurately enough so that we can take advantage of this, our second chance.

For the very elderly whose choices are limited by frailty, there is still a very special and extraordinarily difficult work to be done. I was at a religious conference a year or so ago when a speaker described a woman confined to a nursing home who had found this work and did it daily. It sounds simple at first, but think about. This woman made sure that she showed appreciation for all the services rendered her by the staff, some of whom were less than solicitous, less than pleasant, no doubt weary. She regularly smiled, she thanked every one of the staff, she never complained unnecessarily, and she was friendly without being an incessant chatterbox. Of course, all the staff came to like her, which in turn made her life easier. She had no other choice of work, but she could have just done as many do—complain, suffer loudly, and become depressed. She resisted the easy course and found that she was able to accept and embrace her "work"; and so she received its blessing.

I suspect—but I do not know for sure, because the speaker who told about her did not say—that this fine elderly lady was also able to inspire some laughter in her nursing home. If so, she was both giver and receiver of the ordinary but invaluable twin blessings of laughter and work. How encouraging and hopeful to think that these blessings remain available to us throughout life.

◆　　　◆　　　◆

If this chapter was a bit "different," wait until the next, where I get slightly far out, but not so far that I haven't plenty of company among theologians and other writers. Animals and angels, like laughter and work, can have their good and bad side. Most angels that people have encountered are of the good kind. They will be a bright and fun note on which to end this book.

DISCUSSION QUESTIONS

How do you react to the opening quotation of this chapter, with its bitter undertone? Is it usually true? When is it not true?

Have you ever thought about Jesus laughing, or pictured him that way? Even smiling?

Who tend to be your favorite people? Those who can make you laugh or perhaps those who will listen to you?

Have you ever felt panicked, or at least very uneasy, about facing a day when you have no idea about what you will do?

Do you, for the most part, enjoy whatever is your "work," both paid and unpaid? Would you miss it if you could no longer do it? Does it an any way respond to your own "deepest wanting"?

15

ANIMALS and ANGELS

> I always say that the essence of being a skeptic is not just to question everything and anything, but to believe that anything and everything can be possible. That's the way I feel about angels, that's the way I feel about God, that's the way I feel about an afterlife. [Nuland, quoted by Hauck, 242]

Like laughter and work in the previous chapter, animals and angels may at first seem an odd combination. Admittedly, the differences between animals and angels are more obvious than the similarities. Animals we can see, touch, hear, often smell, and—for those of us who are meat eaters—taste; and no one doubts their existence. Angels, on the other hand, are not demonstrably perceptible to our five senses in most cases; and many of us doubt their existence as individual entities. Much depends on how the word "angel" is defined.

The primary similarity that led me to put animals together with angels in this chapter is that both sometimes serve as spiritual messengers, revealing the nature of the creator in terms of love, power, and mystery. A secondary similarity is that in our minds each fills a space, animals being "below" us and above inanimate nature, and angels being "above" us in the tremendous gap we perceive between humankind and God, the Mystery, the Spirit, the Creator, the Ground of Being. Still another similarity is that both animals and angels have stirred the human imagination since the beginning of time, sometimes even combined with each other. And of course there are what we tend to view as good animals and bad animals, and good angels and bad angels, our judgment depending of course on how these creatures, imaginary or not, affect our lives.

I confess to being what is often termed an "animal nut." I have owned—or more accurately, provided food and shelter for—quite a variety of animals, depending on my family circumstances at a particular time. I presently feed and protect only one dog, one cat, and two horses, species that are all very different in their natures and responses to human beings. Every program about animals on television captures me. I can sit for hours engrossed in the lives of whatever animals are being discussed and shown. I marvel at the fantastic photography that is now possible, so that one can see, close up, birds hatching in nests within trees, bears suckling their young way back in their dens, and monkeys cavorting above the tree canopy in tropical rain forests. How all this is possible I don't—and need not—understand, but I am aware and appreciate that technological advances, ingenuity, and the long hours spent by nature and animal photographers have enabled us to understand a tremendous amount about many animals that heretofore was hidden. So when I write about animals in a book about spirituality and religion, I write not in any sense as a biologist or someone with career experience and knowledge, but rather as an intelligent and attentive recipient of the experience and knowledge of many other people. To these I add my comparatively limited hands-on contact with animals and my fascination with trying to discover and interpret their spiritual significance to us humans.

First we have to go back to that procession of animals leading from inanimate nature to human beings, and acknowledge that the animals filling that void are not separated from us by a very clear line. The traditional demarcation has to do with consciousness in its meaning of being aware of oneself, and then being able to imagine what another creature is thinking and feeling. It has been clearly shown and widely accepted by now that some of the apes share some degree of this type of consciousness with human beings. Other animals with a high degree of intelligence, such as dolphins and elephants, also seem to have such capabilities.

Having spoken against drawing clear lines, I will draw one or two very fuzzy ones at this point for convenience. Animals can be divided roughly into wild animals and domestic animals. Oddly enough, that same fuzzy line between the wild and domestic is very close to the line between those animals that what we consider bad or good. There seems to be an in-between section of wild animals who are also "good" in the minds of many people. These are the ones we have little reason to fear or who cause us no harm, either because we have learned how to avoid the dangers or problems they present or because we have learned to control them without at the same time domesticating them. Otters and deer would be examples, although both present problems to certain groups of people. And those people who have had intimate contact with and learned the habits of almost any wild animal, even such creatures as snakes and crocodiles, do not make the distinction because they no longer fear them.

Dispensing with the subjective and individualistic—as well as irrational—concept of bad and good animals, let us first consider wild animals and what spiritual significance they may have for us. Most observations will also be applicable to domestic (including farm animals) when we leave out of consideration their relationship to us.

What I think most fascinates us is the "otherness" of animals, particularly the wild ones, but also some of the domestic ones. I can look into the eyes of my horses and watch them in the pasture almost endlessly, attracted not only by their beauty and grace but by their being in such a different psychological world from mine. I came upon two interesting and poetic comments that express this otherness compellingly.

> We need another and a wiser and perhaps a more mystical conception of animals…. For the animal shall not be measured by man. In a world older and more complete than ours they move finished and complete, gifted with extensions of the senses we have lost or never

attained, living by voices we shall never hear. They are not brethren, they are not underlings; they are other nations, caught with ourselves in the net of life and time, fellow prisoners of the splendour and travail of the earth. [Henry Beston, 24-25]

I like Beston's phrase, "other nations," which is the sense we have when we look into the eyes of almost any animal. We feel that animals live in a world entirely different from ours, far less complex although often much more dangerous. Their perfect fit into their world is the theme of Scott Russell Sanders:

Animals seem to fill their skins, trees their bark, rivers their banks, so beautifully, that we cannot help but see in their wildness a perfect at-homeness. The words *holy* and *healthy* have the same root, which means *whole*. We perceive in nature an integrity which is our birthright, a unity in which we already participate, in which we cannot help but participate. [Sanders, 166]

And yet, on what is the world of animals based except the struggle for survival of themselves individually, their descendants, and their species? For all predators, that means killing other animals. The repugnance and unacceptability of this idea to people throughout the ages, and not just to "civilized" people, is emphasized by Joseph Campbell: "One of the main problems of mythology is reconciling the mind to this brutal precondition of all life, which lives by the killing and eating of life." [Campbell, 55] Note, however, that it is rare for an animal to kill and eat another of its own species, although this sometimes does occur, particularly among fish and reptiles. The situation changes, however, further up the ladder toward human beings, as socialization and interdependence within the species increases. Various species of ape in some instances will kill each other, even their descendants, much as we humans might, because of inimical relationships or covetousness, either for food or mating rights.

The precariousness of life in the wild comes through loud and clear from those who follow animals' lives closely, wiping away the sentimentality expressed in Walt Whitman's famous lines about their ideal life.

> I could turn and live with animals, they are so placid and self-con-
> tained,
>> I stand and look at them long and long;
>> They do not sweat and whine about their condition.
>> They do not lie awake in the dark and weep for their sins.
>> Not one is dissatisfied, not one is demented with the mania of
> owning things,
>> Not one kneels to another, nor to his kind that lived thousands
> of years ago.
>> Not one is respectable or unhappy over the whole earth.
>> [Walt Whitman, "Song of Myself," section 32]

Whitman obviously lived before the animal specials on television! And I suspect he never had any animals of his own, or if he did, he paid no attention to them. What he is really describing, of course, is his dream of a perfect human life, so different from the reality.

The last two lines of the Whitman poem lead into another aspect of animal behavior that tends not to please us: dominance. One does not need television specials to realize that for all animals dominance is the name of the game. No two animals live together or meet without deciding the question of who is boss. Individuals in certain species may simply decide to stay apart, each in his own territory, but then they carefully mark that territory to avoid confrontations. Within any group, however, the pecking order must be established. It may change, but usually not without a fight.

Many of us prefer not to perceive this dominance struggle among our domestic animals, but it is there. All we have to do is watch a herd of horses for a little while, and soon it becomes clear who is who. I have a gentle, quiet palomino horse that can be ridden by anyone, but woe to any other horse in his pasture who even *thinks* about eating hay in a particular manger or drinking water from a shared bucket at the moment when he even *might* want it. Flat back go his ears, and if the other horse doesn't get the message and trot quickly out of his way, he charges with bared teeth, which sometimes hit their mark on the other horse's rump. Perhaps, in Whitman's words, he is "demented with the mania of owning things!" At the least he is demanding that any other horse symbolically "kneel" to him. This horse, so dominant with his own kind, must have learned as a colt that he is subservient to all human beings. He has never in any way challenged me, although he might briefly suggest to an inexperienced rider that he would like to do his own thing.

Even among amiable dogs who seem to be pals, one has the dominant position and establishes a line that cannot be crossed. They are pals only as long as the line is respected. People tend to think the dominant animal is being nasty and to pity the poor little one in the subservient position, but that is misplaced sympathy. The subservient one usually seems content once his position has been determined. There is no good and bad between and among animals, only more or less dominant.

So what does the "wild kingdom" (the name of an early television series) have to tell about God the creator? Nothing much that we want to hear, but a lot that we need to hear. I doubt if any of us, brought up with the idea of good and evil, would have made such a universe. Life for wild animals (as well as for many domestic ones) is no picnic. It is usually short and brutal. It is dog eat dog among the predators, which of course include humans. What we learn—once again—is that we cannot understand the ways of God.

The problem of why God has created animals, for whom there is no good and evil, to prey upon each other and cause each other to suffer is not a new subject to theologians. C. S. Lewis has an entire chapter on the subject in his short book, *The Problem of Pain*. He points out first of all that whatever we say about "beasts" is speculative; and then he begins to speculate quite broadly. He writes that it is "certainly difficult to suppose that the apes, the elephant, and the higher domestic animals, have not, in some degree, a self or soul which connects experi-

ences and gives rise to rudimentary individuality." [Lewis, *Pain*, 133]
He gets a bit far out with the idea of the fall and evil, and then suggests, on the basis of his cat and dog living peaceably together in his
house, that it "may have been one of man's functions to restore peace
to the animal world," a notion that animals might find laughable (that
is, if they could find ideas laughable to begin with). Lewis moves on
boldly to immortality for domestic animals, which he thinks depends
on their "selfhood" and on their relationship to their masters.

I most certainly do not swallow all this whole, but I am slow to
throw out wholesale anything that a man so perceptive and intuitive as
C. S. Lewis suggests. My marginal notes to this chapter, jotted down
when I first read it in my early twenties, suggest amusement as well as a
high degree of skepticism. Now, in my later and perhaps wiser years,
there are not only amusement and skepticism, but also a sense that
Lewis has hold of something real, but that perhaps he has worked on it
too hard with that restless, imaginative, and pedantic intelligence of
his, all wrapped up in Scripture.

What I harvest from C. S. Lewis and my own experience is first, of
course, that we really can't know with any certainty whatever anything
about an animal's soul and immortality, and further that we don't need
to know. However, I am caught very fast by the idea that some of the
higher animals, with consciousness, have indeed an identity that can be
termed a soul, a self; and furthermore that we perceive that soul in its
relationship to us. It takes no theologian or animal behavior specialist
to come to this conclusion. In fact, anyone with any sensitivity at all
who looks hard into the eyes of a domestic dog or an ape in the zoo
must come away with the sense that "someone is home" in there. Not
so with a sheep or a cow, I have noticed.

I was surprised and pleased to find that the eminent theologian
Martin Buber, hardly the sentimental type, came to the same conclusion, which he expresses within his own world view:

> An animal's eyes have the power to speak a great language. Inde-
> pendently, without needing co-operation of sounds and gestures,

most forcibly when they rely wholly on their glance, the eyes express the mystery in its natural prison, the anxiety of becoming. This condition of the mystery is known only by the animal, it alone can disclose it to us—and this condition only lets itself be disclosed, not fully revealed. The language in which it is uttered is what it says—anxiety, the movement of the creature between the realms of vegetable security and spiritual venture. This language is the stammering of nature at the first touch of spirit, before it yields to spirit's cosmic venture that we call man. But no speech will ever repeat what that stammering knows and can proclaim. [Buber, 96-97]

It turns out that Martin Buber had a cat, or at least had the acquaintance of one. I was once privileged to hear him give a speech years ago in a church in Washington, D.C., and the very idea of this dignified, poetic old man, with his complex theological theories of relationships, looking into a cat's eyes really amuses and amazes me. But why not, after all? At any rate, I have to give you one more quote from him that incorporates this cat:

Sometimes I look into a cat's eyes…. there enters the glance, in its dawn and continuing in its rising, a quality of amazement and of inquiry that is wholly lacking in the original glance with all its anxiety. The beginning of this cat's glance lighting up under the touch of my glance, indisputably questioned me: "It is possible that you think of me? Do you really not just want me to have fun? Do I concern you? Do I exist in your sight? Do I really exist?…" The world of *It* surrounded the animal and myself, for the space of a glance the world of *Thou* had shone out from the depths, to be at once extinguished and put back into the world of *It*. [Buber, 97-98]

There seems indeed to be some soul, some self, in certain animals that is either there without regard to a relationship with humans, as in some of the apes, or perhaps solely developed in response to us, as in cats, dogs, and horses. I very much like Buber's description of that evolutionary response as "the movement of the creature between the realms of vegetable security and spiritual venture," as well as his phrasing for its attempt to communicate with us, "the stammering of nature at the first touch of spirit." Of course, we cannot know with any certainty if all animals have some conscious selfhood, perhaps in a form we cannot recognize.

I draw a specific and practical conclusion from the experience of special relationship that we humans form with certain animals. It is simple and obvious: we must care for and not kill for food or sport those animals with whom such a relationship has been formed. There is a bond of consciousness that prohibits it, and in our deepest selves we know this. It has to do with not killing our own species, because in a sense an animal whose consciousness we acknowledge, no matter how uncertainly, becomes one of us. Exactly what "caring for" is required depends upon the circumstances, as it does between humans.

There is still a third spiritual element revealed to us by animals. We have noted that through their otherness and their predation they reinforce the impossibility of our understanding the ways of the creator. We have speculated that through their budding consciousness they call into being our relationship with them which must bring some limitations with it. The third element comes from only a few species, but it is extremely important to many human lives. These few carry a message of love to those who feel unloved, a large and weary crew any time of the day or night. Primarily this is done by the dog, but also by other animals who live with us or near us, such as cats and horses. You will note that these special carriers of love are not those animals that we have found to be the most intelligent. Some dogs, cats, and horses have a high degree of certain aspects of intelligence peculiar to their breed, but they have not compared in testing to chimpanzees and dolphins, for example.

A dog, like all other animals that develop a relationship with a human being, lives in more than one world. He does not relinquish his membership in the animal kingdom. When out of our control, free of the leash or our voice of command, he will chase and kill a rabbit if he so pleases; and upon seeing another dog, he will race toward it and, forgetting all our human ideas of politeness, enter into the canine form of acquaintance. He will sniff the nose and the tail of the other dog, and if satisfied that there is no immediate challenge, suggest play. After killing and perhaps eating a bit of the rabbit, and after playing according to canine rules with his new acquaintance, he will return and lay his head on our lap, looking up devotedly into our face. We are an important addition to his life, but we do not wipe out the rest of his animal life. We are to him the dominant figure in his pack (which may consist of only the two of us) when we are present. We are the source of his food and shelter and have perhaps become very important to him emotionally, but we have in no way eliminated his animal nature once he is free of us.

In the simple, everyday scenario above, the dog has first killed as a predator; then discussed dominance with another dog, beast to beast; and finally come to us with love as our obedient and devoted friend. Unconsciously, he has acted out the harshness, the otherness, and the love in the universe.

Dogs can so clearly be messengers of love. Norris tells of a seventh-grade child who put it best: "I find God through dogs, because dogs are full of love." [Norris, 109, from James Martin, ed. *How Can I Find God?*] The best of our domestic dogs perfectly fit the job description we would present to God if dogs had not yet been created: A creature who will always give us love and remain with us, regardless of how we treat her; who will respond willingly to all our requests if within her mental and physical power; who is able and pleased to work beside us as herder, retriever, protector, scout, sled dog, guide, companion, and whatever else we can imagine; and who furthermore can delight us by her beauty, grace, and athletic prowess. A dog has to be considered one of the most valuable gifts of the creation to human beings.

Perhaps—probably—undoubtedly, the most important quality the dog has to offer us is love, because that is what we most long for, what we most need to make us whole. Dogs, like God, can and do love the unlovable, and in so doing become channels and messengers of his love. They work at it, too. Dogs will cock their heads to one side, look hard at us, and try to figure out what it is we want of them. They try to learn our language and succeed amazingly well. I am sure you have heard dog owners rave proudly, saying "My dog understands every word I say." Yes, well. At least the dogs try to figure out what it is we want or are going to do, from our intonation, some individual words, and most of all our body language, this being their first key to their own species.

I must say that most people don't hold up their own side when it comes to communicating with dogs. Dogs try to learn our language, but few of us try to make it easy for them. We will use three or four different phrases at different times, all meaning one thing. We will give a command without using their names first, to alert them to the fact that our "blah-blah-blah" is directed to them, and then wonder that they don't jump to it.

And many of us make no attempt at all to learn their language. Dogs, being dogs, wish to have the dominance bit settled, but we humans change our signals from time to time as to who is dominant. We will try to be kind and do "it" their way, whatever "it" is, while they are waiting for their dominant mistress to make a decision and give a command. This is confusing, to say the least. Or we will say "no" in a sweet, kindly way, perhaps even laughing, and expect them to obey. To the dog, who learned from her mother that the negative is given strongly and severely, this "no" means "yes." Dogs welcome clarity. They want to do what we wish, but we—we of the big brain—often neither speak our own language clearly to them nor use their language. Of course, they forgive us or, more probably, they just take what we give them without realizing how much more we could give if we put our minds to it.

Dogs, as messengers of love and protection, as beings devoted to the care of mankind, may be considered a kind of angel. Here is the major connection in the chapter head. People may doubt the existence of angels, but no one doubts the existence of dogs and their love and devotion to people throughout the world.

Let us put aside the question of whether or not angels "really exist" until we have clarified what is meant by the word "angel." I have perused considerable angel literature to find a sufficiently inclusive definition. This one from the Shorter Oxford English Dictionary on Historical Principles is typical of that in most dictionaries: "A ministering spirit or divine messenger; one of an order of spiritual beings superior to man in power and intelligence, who are the attendants and messengers of the Deity." [quoted by Burnham, 80] Thomas Aquinas, giving a series of fifteen lectures on angels at the University of Paris in 1259, said that angels are "all intellect." [Burnham, 167] His lectures formed the basis of "angelology" for the next 800 years, according to Sophy Burnham, who researched the subject thoroughly. Meister Eckhart, in the fourteenth century, agreed with him, writing that "That's all an angel is, an idea of God." [quoted by Burnham, 56] In the nineteenth century, Mary Baker Eddy writes that "Angels are pure thoughts from god.... Angels are God's representatives." [quoted by Burnham, 49] These quotations seem to imply that angels are somehow a matter of the intellect, but they refer to the mind of God, not of people. People who have experienced angels are never talking about intellectual experiences.

We have to start with angels as being at the least a persistent *perception* of humankind, shared in one form or another, and more or less, by people of all cultures, all times, and all religions (although often not central to them). During certain periods, especially the Middle Ages, people seemed fascinated and even obsessed by angels and saw, heard, or felt many of them. Dionysius the Pseudo-Aeropagie in the sixth century even described nine orders of angels, and these were accepted through the eighteenth century, with names and tasks assigned to many of them. We ourselves seem to be in a period of interest in angels, judging from the quantity of books on the subject and the plethora of angel trivia on sale everywhere. Ours, however, rarely have names, nor do we place them in any strict hierarchy. They are mostly personal to individuals.

In recent books there is no standard physical appearance for angels. Some have wings, others do not; many are wearing white robes and seem to have a golden aura, while others are dressed in bright clothing or much the same apparel as the person to whom they are appearing. Angels may be androgens, male, or female and some, although this is comparatively rare, even have sex and children. They almost always bring light and warmth, although many radiate an "unbearable whiteness." Some may even be flesh and blood people (usually strangers) or animals (as in dogs?) who suddenly appear and as suddenly leave after delivering the message or accomplishing a rescue of some sort.

Although much has been written and many illustrations drawn about angels as inhabitants of heaven, our concern is with angels as experienced by human beings. We perceive them as coming to perform specific tasks, usually but not always singly. They are messengers and guardians sent by God to an individual, either for a special reason or as lifelong guardians, particularly for children. According to Sophy Burnham, who bases her conclusions on both her own experiences and those of hundreds of other people, three marks distinguish an angel: It brings "calm and peaceful serenity that descends sweetly over you"; its message is always basically "Fear not;" and its visit is never forgotten, although perhaps it remains untold. [Burnham, 38-40] People have occasionally reported encounters with what they have called "bad angels," but these appear primarily in myths of creation and are part of theories of evil and Satan.

I mentioned in the beginning of this chapter that angels, as we conceive of them, fill a gap in our mental hierarchy between ourselves and God. This idea is born out by the fact that they appear most often and most elaborately in monotheistic religions, whereas polytheistic religions have all sorts of minor gods and goddesses filling the spiritual space between God and us and bringing messages to us and otherwise mingling in our affairs. We seem to need that space filled intellectually, knowing how powerless and unimportant we are in comparison to God, the great Mystery, Creator of the universe. Furthermore, we think it more likely that some spirit not quite so great, not quite so severe, is more likely to condescend to visit us; and we are more comfortable with a lesser spirit—although often in the Bible even angels strike fear in the heart of those to whom they appear.

It seems we humans have our angels because, as a species, we are unable and have always been unable to believe in our heart of hearts that the God of the universe and all creation, of earthquakes and the hurricane, of humanity with its cruelty and evil, and of animal and human predation is also the loving God of Jesus and other sages. It is too much for us. We need lesser gods, a mother god like the Virgin Mary, and angels in familiar and gentle form. These spiritual beings, as intermediaries, bring us our personal messages from the Supreme Being.

St. Augustine writes of angels as no more nor less than spirit messengers, saying that they "are spirit, but it is not because they are spirits that they are angels. They become Angels when they are sent. For the name Angel refers to their office, not their nature. You ask the name of this nature, it is spirit; you ask its office, it is that of an Angel, which is a messenger." [quoted by Burnham, 178]

Not all of us have received such messengers, or, if we have, we have not perceived them as something we would call "angels." Burnham writes:

> It is not that skeptics do not experience the mysterious and divine, but rather that the mysteries are presented to them in such a flat and factual, everyday, reasonable way so as not to disturb; for this is the rule: no one receives more information than he can bear. Therefore it seems that angels bring messages in the form—even in the dialect—that each recipient can hear. [Burnham, 110-11]

We are all different in spiritual capabilities and sensitivities as in other ways—my recurrent theme. Contrast the message-receiving capability imagined for the skeptic above with Burnham's poetic, intuitive, and even nostalgic description of the human situation as felt by those held less fast by their rational faculties:

> We know nothing of this other realm, except that we are given brief, fleeting glimpses in our hearts. We hear its singing in lost memories. We see it at the edge of our eye, but so ephemerally that when we turn to face it, it's already gone. We feel it in our loneliness, the hollow hole at the heart.... It is the existential longing for surcease that makes us believe that something other must exist; for if we remembered nothing, if we had no sense of having once been filled, would we now recognize our present emptiness? [Burnham, 22]

Human beings are a visualizing species of animal. The spiritual movings and perceptions of our soul both affect and are affected by the physical minutiae of our brains. Surgeon, professor, and author Sherwin B. Nuland, whose quotation opened this chapter, considers that angel visits may be explained scientifically as the result of endorphins, morphinelike chemicals produced within the body in occasions of acute distress. The endorphins produce for many people a feeling of serenity and for others even "certain kinds of hallucinatory phenomena." [quoted by Hauck, 237-38] People have evolved this way. The physical "how" of seeing or hearing an angel may thus be endorphins, while the spiritual "why," the meaning, may only be known to an individual.

Everything, literally *everything*, both spiritual and physical, in the world interacts with everything else. How can we possibly separate it all? How can we possibly say what is "real," what actually exists, and what is not real and does not exist? If my eyes were to tell me that I have seen what I perceive as a divine messenger and what I name as an angel, no one would be able to convince me that I have not. And I would be correct, because my perceptions exist, are indeed real. The world of our own spirits and of the Spirit is real, more real than the world of our senses.

So: Do angels "really exist"? Defined as spiritual perceptions, of course. They are of the spiritual realm, perceived as we humans do perceive, in images. Remember the difficulty and yet almost necessity of picturing God himself/herself and of trying to give him/her a name that would not present a limiting picture? So with angels.

I suppose I should confess at this point that I personally have received no specific spiritual message, ever, from anything or anybody that I perceived and would define as an angel. The only possible exception is an odd feeling of certainty I had at the Erving Post Office one morning. I was on my way to Greenfield to visit a client and stopped in to mail a package. I can still visualize the scene clearly. The post office was at that time in a white trailer. I entered and had to wait a moment while another woman was finishing her apparently casual conversation with the postmistress. I just heard the end of the conversation, and I don't even remember what it was about. I made some casual remark to both women, just a pleasantry, and the other customer—dumpy, with white hair—looked at me and smiled; then left. Immediately I said to myself, "That woman was an angel. I know it.... Good heavens, have I seen an angel?" How that fits into all I have been saying about angels, I don't know. This lady was for sure made of flesh and blood. If an angel in any sense, she was a person serving perhaps unknowingly as a messenger of the Spirit. However, I was not aware of having received any message, about my clients or anything at all in my life. As I have looked back on the scenario, the only message could have been: "Wake up. There are more things in heaven and earth than are dreamed of in your philosophy" (with thanks to Hamlet and W.S.). But I already knew that, or thought I did.

All that personal incident adds to this discussion of angels is the information that I am not speaking as an "angel person." I am not one of those spiritually and intuitively sensitive persons who receive spiritual messages from what they visually or aurally perceive as an "angel."

So why write about angels? Do they matter? I think angels do matter to us in that those who have seen them and tell us about them bear witness to the tremendous flow of spiritual activity constantly occurring in the world of which we may not be aware. The message that angels give us, whether or not we think we have seen or heard one, is that the Spirit is active in this world, that it is a Spirit of love for each one of us. They tell us all to awaken and fear not.

We may not ourselves perceive the Spirit in the form of angels, but we must acknowledge and ponder the obvious fact that others do and have for centuries. And that should alert us to watch for the Spirit as we ourselves individually are able to perceive that Spirit in our lives, carrying the message to each of us that God, the Mystery, the Ground of our Being, does cherish us, you and me.

And that is the name of the game, that is indeed "where it's at." That *is* what matters, what can make life tolerable, fascinating, exciting, and finally even joyful.

DISCUSSION QUESTIONS

Has the devotion of a dog or cat ever brought you out of a bad mood and made you happier? Do you think that the love an animal expresses for a person is an emanation of the Spirit of love?

Has the killing among animals and the brutally short life they live in the wild ever given you second thoughts about the loving nature of the creator? How do you reconcile the two, or can't you do so?

What animals, if any, is it ethical to kill for food or for the preservation of a species?

Have you ever experienced an angel visitation? If so, what was it like? Did you get a message from it? Did it in any way change your life?

Has anyone you know ever told you about an angel visitation? If so, how did you react—with scorn, skepticism, jealousy, interest, or in some other way?

ANNOTATED BIBLIOGRAPHY

The listings preceded by an asterisk (*) may be especially interesting and helpful in coming to an understanding and experience of the "here-and-nowness" of the Spirit.

Berry, Wendell. *Jayber Crow*. Washington, D.C.: Counterpoint, 2000. 363 pp. The author describes the book as "the life story of Jayber Crow, Barber, of the Port William membership, as written by himself." Abounding with remarkable characters, this novel is a lyrical love story, a celebration of compassion and community, and a philosophical exploration all in one. Berry is a poet, essayist, and novelist.

———*A World Lost*. Washington, D.C.: Counterpoint, 1996. 151 pp. Narrated by Andy Catlett, this novel traces his gradual coming to terms with the murder of his uncle when he was nine years old in Kentucky. Berry brings Andy to the conclusion that compassion is possible when understanding is not. People and places are portrayed with exceptional sensitivity.

Beston, Henry. *Outermost House: A Year of Life on the Great Beach of Cape Cod*. New York: Henry Holt and Co., 1992. 218 pp. First published in 1928. This journal of a year spent alone in a house on a Cape Cod beach is considered a classic in U.S. nature writing. In 1964 the house was officially proclaimed a National Literary Landmark, but in 1978 it was swept out to sea by a winter storm.

*Borg, Marcus J. *The God We Never Knew: Beyond Dogmatic Religion to a More Authentic Contemporary Faith.* San Francisco: HarperSanFrancisco, 1997. 182 pp. Borg describes this book as "an attempt to do Christian theology within the framework of religious pluralism and the cross-cultural study of religion." He interprets Christian traditions at a deeper level, so that they acquire spiritual significance for everyday life. The author is a secular Jesus scholar.

*——*Meeting Jesus Again for the First Time: The Historical Jesus & the Heart of Contemporary Faith.* San Francisco: HarperSanFrancisco, 1994. 150 pp. This scholarly yet clear and accessible book moves from the author's skeptical approach to Christianity as a young man to his mature understanding of Jesus the man and of the nature of faith. Borg makes a distinction between the pre-Easter and the post-Easter Jesus.

*Buber, Martin. *I and Thou.* New York: Macmillan Publishing Company, 1987. 137 pp. First published in 1958. Translated by Ronald Gregor Smith. In this classic theological work, Buber discusses in a poetic and sometimes contradictory fashion the heart of the relationship between God and a person. He contrasts the I-Thou relationship to the more usual I-It situation.

Burnham, Sophy. *A Book of Angels: Reflections on Angels Past and Present and True Stories of How They Touch Our Lives.* New York: Ballantine Books, 1990. 301 pp. Both a spiritual memoir and an introduction to the literature on angels, this book combines historical research and reports of personal angel encounters. Although not the first popular book on the subject, it sparked a spate of others about angels.

*Campbell, Joseph, with Bill Moyers. *The Power of Myth.* New York: Doubleday, 1988. 231 pp. This illustrated book contains an edited transcript of the conversation between Joseph Campbell and Bill Moyers for the filming of the six-hour PBS series of the same title. Campbell taught for almost forty years as an instructor at Sarah Lawrence College, and Moyers is an acclaimed journalist. Their discussion centers on myth and includes many fascinating stories on a variety of subjects, such as marriage, savior figures, sacrifice, eternity, and heroes.

Coles, Robert. *The Secular Mind*. Princeton, N.J.: Princeton University Press, 1999. 189 pp. A research psychiatrist at Harvard University, Coles traces the history of the secular mind, as opposed to the spiritual being, from biblical times to the present, with speculation about the future. Persons quoted and discussed include Dietrich Bonhoeffer, Dorothy Day, Paul Tillich, Sigmund and Anna Freud, William Carlos Williams, Flannery O'Connor, and Walker Percy. Coles considers the current faith that the human brain can explore and finally control our psychological life fully.

The Dalai Lama. *Ethics for the New Millenium*. New York: Riverhead Books, 1999. 237 pp. Written in a rather simplistic and repetitive style, this discussion of ethics maintains that only love and compassion are required to lead a happy life. Nevertheless, it is clear that the Dalai Lama believes that religion is helpful. His other recent books differ little from this one.

*Dillard, Annie. "For the Time Being," in Notre Dame Magazine, *The Best American Essays 1999*. pp. 74-89. This essay is a passionate, poetic, and outspoken discussion of attempts to reconcile the evil and disasters of this world with the omnipotence and love of God. Offering pithy quotations from those who have wrestled with this problem earlier, author Dillard admits that we cannot provide an answer, but only "live completely in the world."

Gallagher, Nora. *Things Seen and Unseen: A Year Lived in Faith*. New York: Vintage Books, 1998. 241 pp. Organized by the seasons of the Christian calendar, this account of magazine writer Gallagher's year of active participation in an Episcopal church in California describes her gradual conversion. Volunteer work in the Kitchen sponsored by the church brought her into close contact with a wide variety of people and was pivotal in her spiritual journey.

Gallagher, Winifred. *Working on God.* New York: Random House, 1999. 340 pp. A reporter of behavioral science and author, Gallagher spent time in a Zen monastery, a cloistered convent, and a Conservative synagogue that shares a Christian church. Told as a personal journey, this narrative depicts the broad-based spiritual movement the author believes is transforming culture as well as religion.

Goodall, Jane, with Phillip Berman. *Reason for Hope: A Spiritual Journey.* New York: Warner Books, 1999. 282 pp. In this memoir, Goodall, known worldwide for her work with chimpanzees, tells how her experiences developed her awareness of the "Spiritual Power" around us all.

*Hart, Thomas. *Spiritual Quest: A Guide to the Changing Landscape.* Mahwah, NJ: Paulist Press, 1999. 180 pp. As both a theologian and therapist, Hart is here writing for contemporary people who are aware of their spiritual hunger but are disillusioned with or have never understood traditional Christianity. His emphasis throughout is on the presence of God in all our life experiences, "in the depths of all Reality." This book provides an unusually perceptive, clearly written, and accessible discussion of spiritual issues.

Hauck, Rex, ed., *Angels: The Mysterious Messengers.* New York: Ballantine Books, 1994. 316 pp. This is the companion volume to an NBC television series in which Hauck interviewed fifteen contemporary authors about their opinion of the nature of angels. Physician Sherwin B. Nuland was among those interviewed, as was angel enthusiast Sophy Burnham, one of whose books is listed above.

*James, William. *The Varieties of Religious Experience.* With an introduction by theologian Reinhold Niebuhr. New York: Collier Books, 1961. 416 pp. First published in 1902. This sometimes difficult but fascinating and encyclopedic discussion of religious experience (based on lectures at the University of Edinburgh) is a "must-read" for any serious student of the spiritual life. Writing as a psychologist, James has "loaded the lectures with concrete examples," including some that are extreme. He warns throughout that we must not confuse facts and experiences with their meaning and value, and concludes that, because religious experiences are as different as the people who have them, we should be tolerant.

Lamott, Anne. *Travelling Mercies: Some Thoughts on Faith.* New York: Anchor Books, 2000. 275 pp. This very personal, candid, and humorous story of novelist Anne Lamott's struggle toward faith is set in the context of her joining a community of faith in a Presbyterian church in California.

*Lewis, C. S. *The Horse and His Boy.* New York: The Macmillan Co., 1954. 191 pp. The fifth among the famous children's series, *The Chronicles of Narnia,* this is a tale of the boy Shasta and his horse, Bree. The central figure of all the chronicles is the lion Aslan, who symbolically stands for Jesus. For its interest as an analogy, its wisdom, and its narrative appeal, this book is a delight for adults to read to children. Lewis was Professor of Medieval and Renaissance English at Cambridge University as well as a prolific and well-known author on theological subjects.

*——*Letters to Malcolm: Chiefly on Prayer.* New York: Harcourt Brace Jovanovich, Inc., 1963. 124 pp. Writing to the Malcolm to whom the famous *The Screwtape Letters* were addressed, Lewis

humorously and perceptively discusses the practical aspects of prayer.

*——*Miracles: A Preliminary Study.* New York: Macmillan Publishing Co., Inc., 1947. 192 pp. In this book, Lewis examines in a logical fashion the philosophical questions concerning the possibility and probability that miracles happen, while pointing out the dangers of a preconceived conclusion.

*——*The Problem of Pain.* New York: Macmillan Publishing Co., Inc., 1962. 160 pp. The paperback cover describes the content of this book as follows: "The intellectual problem raised by human suffering, examined with sympathy and realism." The description is on the mark.

Norris, Kathleen. *Amazing Grace: A Vocabulary of Faith.* New York: Riverhead Books, 1998. 384 pp. Both a series of essays on "scary" Christian terms and a memoir of a spiritual journey, this book deals with the value of group worship and religious tradition in acquiring a "lived faith." Norris writes both poetry and nonfiction works about her spiritual life.

Nouwen, Henri J. M. *Reaching Out: The Three Movements of the Spiritual Life.* New York: Image Books, 1986. 165 pp. A well-known writer on the spiritual life and a Catholic priest, Nouwen describes a quest for "authentic" spirituality as a movement from loneliness to solitude, then from hostility to hospitality, and finally from illusion to prayer. The book contains many little gems that compensate for its unfamiliar approach.

Ozick, Cynthia. "The Impious Impatience of Job," from *The American Scholar,* reprinted in *The Best American Essays 1999,* ed. Edward Hoagland. New York: Houghton Mifflin Co., 1999. pp. 201-11. This brief essay is a perceptive and powerful analysis of the Book of Job. Ozick is an essayist, novelist, and writer of short stories.

Price, Reynolds. "Jesus of Nazareth then and Now," *Time*, December 6, 1999. pp. 86-94. This article briefly examines historical research about Jesus, explains the author's attempt to portray Jesus's life in his 1996 book, *Three Gospels,* and provides short narrative accounts of "pregnant situations." *Three Gospels* includes a new translation of Mark, another of John, and one of his own. Price is a biblical scholar as well as a prolific writer of many kinds of literature.

Provine, Robert R. *Laughter: A Scientific Investigation.* New York: Penguin Putnam Inc., 2000. 258 pp. A ten-year project led to this book by Dr. Provine, professor of psychology and neuroscience at the University of Maryland, Baltimore County. It presents an erudite, witty, and sometimes surprising examination of laughter, including its evolution, role in social relationships, contagiousness, neural mechanisms, and health benefits.

Sanders, Scott Russell. *Staying Put: Making a Home in a Restless World.* Boston: Beacon Press, 1993. 203 pp. An essayist and teacher of literature at Indiana University, Sanders tells his personal story of learning the spiritual advantage of "staying put" in one place, of establishing and committing to a home. His philosophical approach to living includes a strong feeling for nature and deep concern for the environment.

Shields, Carol. *Larry's Party.* London: Fourth Estate Limited, 1998. 339 pp. First published in 1997. A fictional account of what it may be like to be a man in the late twentieth century, this novel is absorbing, perceptive, and beautifully structured. The dinner party at the end has been highly praised by critics.

Spong, Shelby. *Why Christianity Must Change or Die: A Bishop Speaks to Believers in Exile.* San Francisco: HarperSanFrancisco, 1998. 257 pp. Bishop Spong proposes a "new reformation of the church's faith and practice," emphasizing his theological departure from "theism," while also arguing that he properly remains within the Christian church. His many cogent observations in this book help to make up for his insistence on his self-declared status as an "exile." He has received considerable attention from the media.

*Watts, Alan W. *Behold the Spirit: A Study in the Necessity of Mystical Religion.* New York: Pantheon Books Inc., 1947. 254 pp. The theme is that we meet God, indeed find union with God, in the "Eternal Now." Watts discusses the current low ebb of "Church religion," in which he thinks that the meaning of religion is being confused with its form. He considers the Incarnation in various perspectives, trying to infuse doctrine and practice with the reality of spiritual experience. Alan Watts, a former Anglican priest, became an exponent of Zen Buddhism. This is an inspirational—if at times repetitive and difficult—theological book.

ABOUT THE AUTHOR

Helen Hills, a Wellesley College graduate, lives in New England, where she works with the elderly. Her books of practical wisdom have found many grateful readers.

0-595-29454-5